ISLAM
AND CIVILIZATION

SYED ABUL HASAN ALI NADWI

Translation of the Qur'ān

It should be perfectly clear that the Qur'ān is only authentic in its original language, Arabic. Since perfect translation of the Qur'ān is impossible, we have used the translation of the meaning of the Qur'ān throughout the book, as the result is only a crude meaning of the Arabic text.

Qur'ānic verses appear in speech marks proceeded by a reference to the Surah and verse number. Sayings (Hadith) of Prophet Muhammad (saw) appear in inverted commas along with reference to the Hadith Book and its Reporter.

This work is

DEDICATED

to the

Centre of Islamic Studies

at

St. Cross College,
University of Oxford. (U. K.)

CONTENTS

In the name of Allah, the most beneficent, the most Merciful.

INTRODUCTION

I was first invited to present a paper on Islam and civilization in connection with the fifteenth century celebrations
(which were organized[1] in different ways in various Muslim
countries) organized by the National Council for Arts and
Culture under the Ministry of Information, Kuwait. I felt
inclined to accept the invitation since I was myself aware of
the significance of the subject and had touched upon it briefly
in my writings. I prepared a paper for the occasion.

The meeting in which this paper was read was held in the
hall of the Science College on Wednesday, Safar 18, 1404/
November 23, 1983 under the aegis of the Ministry of Information, Kuwait. It was attended by a large number of distinguished persons, scholars and notables. This paper was also
presented in another meeting organized by Al-Nādi al-Thaqāfi
of Makkah on Safar 30,1404/ December 6, 1983 and later on
included in a collection of my articles[2].

The paper included several salient points which were
thought-provoking, but it was still brief, since I had not been

---

1. One of it was the meeting organized by Muslim Students on Ist November 1980 (Dhil Hijja 22, 1400) in the Ganga Prasad Memorial Hall at
   Lucknow. My address in that meeting has since been published as
   "The fifteenth Century" in English, Arabic and Urdu and was, warmly
   received in literary circles.
2. *Ahādith Sariha Ma Ikhwānena al-Arab wal-Muslimeen,* Dārul 'Arafāt,
   Rae Bareli.

able to devote adequate time to expand it owing to my heavy engagements. I was again asked by the Fourth International Conference on Seerat to participate in another meeting to be held in the Azhar University, Cairo. One of the topics included in its agenda was the same as mentioned earlier and this helped me to give further thought to the matter. On this occasion I collected material from several books on the subject and dealt with the issues raised in my earlier paper in greater detail in order to highlight the gifts of Islam and the prophethood of Muhammad (peace be upon him) which made it a sort of research treatise. Thus it assumed the shape that it could be found useful by all including such non-Muslim friends who want to know more about Islam.

I have not felt shy of giving extracts of my own earlier writings in this paper if I have found them relevant to the topics discussed in it. The readers would come across such citations from *Islam and the World* and *Muhammad Rasūlullāh* since it would have not been worthwhile to re-write these passages in a different phrase. All these have gone to make it a concise yet thought-provoking work.

The Fourth International Conference on Seerat was, however, postponed but I decided to publish it for the benefit of all those who are either interested in the subject or engaged in the work of Islamic D'awah.

S. ABUL HASAN ALI NADWI

3rd Rajab, 1406
15th March, 1986

1

Scope and Significance

Islam and civilization is a realistic and living issue which relates not only to the prophethood of Muhammad (peace be upon him) and the teachings of Islam, but also to the reality of life itself, the present and future of mankind and the historic role played by Muslims in the development of culture and building up a flourishing civilization. This is a topic important enough to receive attention of an academic body instead of being given thought by a single individual. In its depth and scope it can compare with any standard subject of thought pertaining to life of man. It covers an immense area in time and space, from the first century of Islamic era to this day and from one corner of the world to the other. In its immanence it encompasses from creed to morals and behaviour, individual as well as social, linked with diverse phenomena of life like law, politics, international relations, arts, letters, poetics, architecture, cultural refinement etc. Each of these aspects of human life are indeed many-sided and hence an academic body composed of scholars of different disciplines is required to study them so that each may undertake an objective research and present his detailed findings courageously, without fear or favour. Each of these scholars, specialist in his own field, can discuss the issues in greater detail as, for example, one can study the creed and religious thought in Islam, the other sociology and culture, the third Islamic law, the fourth equality and dignity of man, the fifth the position of women and so on. Detailed discussion on each subject undertaken in this manner can indeed cover an encyclopaedia rather than be dealt with by an individual like me who has little time to spare for literary pursuits,. But as the saying goes the thing which cannot be owned completely should not be given up altogether. I have, in working on this subject, kept in view the Quranic verse which says: "And if no torrent falls on it, then even a gentle rain".[1]

A Delicate Task

Analysis of the ingredients of any developed culture is perhaps a very difficult and delicate task. For the intrinsic constituents of any culture get assimilated over a period of time, these are always elusive and their interaction is difficult to indicate after they have shaped themselves into a wholeness that is known as a society and its culture. They enter into the lives of the people imperceptibly and become a part of its soul and blood ; give it a distinct identity much in the same way as instincts, education and training, circumstances and diet go to make the personality of an individual. No chemical laboratory yet exists which can be helpful in such a historical analysis nor a microscope has been invented so far which can examine minutely the constituent elements of any culture.

The attending difficulties of the task leave the only way and that is an in-depth study of different nations and their cultures so that their past and present may be compared to find out the effects of Islamic teachings and the revolutionary call of the holy Prophet for reformation and guidance of human society.

The part played by this call in reforming or changing the earlier creeds, pagan ways of thought, manners and customs of the ancient world as well as in giving birth to new ideas and values that have helped in giving rise to a new culture and civilization, has to be studied and examined. This is a stupen-

1. Q. 2 : 265

dous task but also rewarding enough to be undertaken by an
academic body in any Islamic country or one of their universities, if not by the organizations like the UNESCO or the more
developed academic centres in Europe or America. There is
not the least doubt that such a research would be more useful
than those in which these universities and literary bodies are
engaged at present.

Difficulties confronting the task

Identification of the influences of Islam on human life
and culture is an extremely difficult task since these influences
have by now become part and parcel of the life and culture
of different nations to an extent that these people cannot
themselves indicate whether they are extrinsic or intrinsic,
borrowed from Islam or evolved by them internally. Many
of these Islamic influences are now the flesh and bone of
their existence and integrated with their modes of thought and
culture.

All-pervasive influence of Islam

Here I would first like to cite a passage from my own
work *Islam and the World* in which I have delineated the
impact of Islamic civlization in shaping attitudes of the people
and their cultural advancement during the heyday of its glory.

"The rejuvenating currents of Islam ran through the world,
infusing men everywhere with a new life and an
unparalleled enthusiasm for progress. The lost values
of life had been discovered. Paganism became a sign
of reaction, while it was considered progressive to be
associated with Islam. Even nations that did not
come directly under the influence of Islam, profoundly,
though unconsciously, benefitted by the freshness and
vitality of the new creative impulses released by its
impact on large parts of the world. Numerous
aspects of their thought and culture bear evidence to
the magic touch of Islam. All the reform movements

that arose in their midst, owed their origin to Islamic influences."[1]

It is well-nigh impossible to enumerate the influence exerted by Islam in different fields and on different nations and countries. We can only make an attempt to describe these in a few spheres where they have played a conspicuous role in the reformation, guidance and progress of humanity towards a better and healthier existence in contradistinction to the norms adopted normally by the Muslims during the period of their decadence. These universal gifts of Islam have been presented in this study under ten headings.

1. Clear and distinct Faith in the Oneness of God.
2. Concept of human unity and equality.
3. Proclamation of human dignity.
4. Raising the position of woman and restoration of her rights.
5. Infusing hope and self-confidence in man.
6. Unification of spirit and matter : truce between the two.
7. Alliance between religion and knowledge.
8. Intellectual pursuit in religious matters.
9. Promotion of morality and justice : a duty enjoined on Muslims.
10. Universal creed and culture.

---

1. S. Abul Hasan Ali Nadwi, *Islam and the World,* Lucknow, 1980, p. 87

2

Clear and distinct faith in the Oneness of God

We would now take up the initial gift of Islam which also constitutes an invaluable heritage of Muhammad (peace be upon him). This is the gift of absolute and undiluted oneness of God, a creed revolutionary, life-giving and vigorous, that cannot be compared with anything man has pinned his faith on, either before or after the prophet of Islam.

Effect of paganism on human life

Man has been proud and presumptuous, boastful of his creations like philosophy and poetry and art of government; he took as much pride in enslaving other countries and nations as in digging canals and turning arid lands into gardens; often he has arrogated himself to the position of God ; but he has also demeaned himself by bowing his head before inanimate, lifeless objects, things of his own creation which could neither harm nor do any favour to him.

> "And if a fly should rob them of aught,
> they would never rescue it. Feeble
> indeed are the seaker and the sought.[1]"

Man prostrated himself before his own creations, feared

---

1. Q. 22 : 73

them and begged them for help. He was over-awed by mountains, rivers, trees, animals and harboured credulous beliefs and had an irrational fear of the demons and devils. He paid divine respect even to reptiles and insects. He spent his life in the fear of the unknown and hope from non-existent powers, all of which went to produce mental confusion, cowardice, doubtfulness and indecision in him. Brahmanic India had shot ahead of every other region in the world with its 33 million gods and goddesses.[1] Everything which fascinated man or appeared frightening was elevated to the position a deity.

Effect of Monotheism on Human life

The Qur'ān and the holy Prophet declared that this universe was neither without a Lord nor was it jointly controlled by a set of deites. It had One Lord and Master, the Creator and Controller wielding complete and absolute power over it. The Qur'ān announced: *Lo ! His is the creation and the Command,*[2] which meant that God was the Sole Creator, the Sole Originator, or, the Sole Creative Principle and everything around man was dependent on Him by virtue of its creation by Him. *Yet to Him submitted whoso is in the Heavens and the earth, willingly or unwillingly*[3], was a natural corollary of this declaration meaning that all things in nature, whether heavenly ones or the earthly, bow down to His decrees and have perforce to submit to His physical laws—so Exalted is He. Then, was it not incumbent on the creature possessing will and option to submit to Him willingly : sincere and exclusive obeisance was due to God alone. He asks : *Belongs not sincere religion to God ?* [4]

The natural consequence following from this belief was that the world was united through a Common Principle; a

1. R. C. Dutt. *Ancient India,*Vol. III. p. 276 and L. S. S. O' Mally, *Popular Hinduism : The Religion of the Masses*, Cambridge, 1935.
2. Q. 7 : 54
3. Q. 3 : 83
4. Q. 39 : 3

Universal Law was running through it. Man was led to acknowledge a unity of purpose, motive and law in the varied phenomena of nature which could also help him to find a meaning
and significance in his own life since it was integral to the
wisdom underlying the integrated nature of this universe.

The Prophet of Islam acquainted man with the clear and
easy creed of the unity of God which was satisfying and full of
vitality since it took away all the irrational fear out of him.
This simple creed made him self-reliant, courageous, rational
and undoubting by removing the fear of everything else save
that of His real Master and Lord. It was because of this creed
that man came to recognise his creator as the Supreme Power,
the Enricher and the Destroyer. This discovery meant a world
of change for him; he could now see the unity of cause in the
manifoldness of phenomena, was reassured of his pivotal position
in the scheme of creation, became aware of his worth and
dignity, in short, his acceptance of the serfdom of One and only
God made him the master of every other created being and
object. As a vicegerent of God, he became aware of the
exalted position allocated to him as the executor of the will of
God on earth. It was a concept unknown to the world earlier.

Effect of Monotheism on other Religions

It was thus the prophethood of Muhammad (peace be upon
him) which granted the gift of absolute monotheism to
humanity. Faith in one and only God was earlier something
most unusual but its forceful advocacy by Islam made it such
a compelling concept that no religion and no social philosophy
remained uninfluenced by it. Even polytheistic religions taking
pride in idol worship and multiplicity of deities started confes-
sing the existence of the Supreme Lord and Master by taking
recourse to philosophical justification for the concept of unity
in multiplicity. They began to feel ashamed of their pantheism,
developed a sense of inferiority complex and started making
efforts to bring their creed closer to Islam.

How the absolute and unalleyod monotheism of Islam

proved to be a revolutionary concept for humanity has been sharply brought out by Syed Sulaimān Nadwi in his *Sīrat-un-Nabi* in these words:

> "The nations which were unfamiliar with the creed of monotheism were also nes ent of the worth and dignity of man : they took man as just a servitor of every natural phenomenon. It was the lesson of monotheism taught by Prophet Muhammad (peace be upon him) that removed the fear of everything save God from the heart of man. This was a revolutionary concept for it pulled down everything—from the sun to the rivers and ponds on earth—from their pedestal of divinity to an attendant in the service of mankind. The magic of regal glory and splendour vanished : monarchs of Babylonia, Egypt, India and Iran no longer remained the lords and the "highest gods". deriving their right and authority from the gods and angels, but became servants and guardians to be appointed by the people themselves."

> "Mankind under the authority of gods and goddesses had been divided into castes and classes, high and low. nobles and menials; some were supposed to have been born of God's mouth, others from his hand or foot. These articles of faith had drawn such lines of demarcation between man and man that he could never hope to be united again. Human equality and brotherhood had perished from the earth converting it into a vast arena for asserting one's superiority and vanity through the most barbarous means, if need be. Then came the belief in monotheism levelling all human beings, destroying all concepts of high and low-born, making them all servants of God, equal in His sight, brother unto one another and having equal rights and obligations. The revolutionary changes that were brought about by this radical creed in social, moral and political fields of human life are self-evident

from the pages of history."

"The truth of this principle was at last acknowledged by those who were not acquainted either with the Oneness of God or the equality of mankind ; who could not get rid of the false notion of their superiority even in the House of God; who discriminated on grounds of wealth, colour and race between men bowing in submission to the same deity, Muslims have been enjoying the fruits of human equality for the last thirteen hundred years solely because of their faith in the Oneness of God. They do not acknowledge any man-made distinctions ; all are servants of the same Lord, all are equals in the sight of God; no dividing line of wealth, race, colour and nationality can now separate them ; only he is worthy of greater honour who is more God-fearing, more obedient to God.[1] *Surely the noble among you in the sight of God is the most God-fearing of you.*[2]

Influence of Islam on India.

The deep imprint Islam left on Indian thought and culture has been discussed by K. M. Pannikar in his *Survey of Indian History* in which he says :

"One thing is clear. Islam had profound effect on Hinduism during this period. Medieval Hindu theism is in some ways a reply to the attack of Islam; and the doctrines of medieval teachers, by whatever names their gods are known, are essentially theistic. It is the one supreme God that is the object of the devotee's adoration and it is to His grace that we are asked to look for redemption. All Bhakti cults are therefore essentially monotheistic, not in the exclusive sense that other devotees cannot worship the same supreme being

1. Syed Sulaiman Nadwi, *Sirat-un-Nabi*, Azamgarh, Vol. IV, pp. 523-24
2. Q. 49 : 13

under other names, but in the affirmative belief that whether known as Siva, Krishna or Devi, they all symbolise the One and the Eternal. This is of course most noticeable in the songs of Kabir,[1] the influence of which was very great among the common folk."[2]

Another well-known scholar, Dr. Tarachand who argues in a similar strain has cited Barth in his support from the *Religions of India*.

"The Arabs of the Khilāfat had arrived on the shores (of South India) in the character of travellers and had established commercial relations and intercourse with these parts long before the Afghans, Turks or Mongols, their co-religionists, came as conquerors. Now, it is precisely in these parts that from the ninth to the twelfth century, those great religious movements took their rise which are connected with the name of Sankara, Rāmānuja, Anandatīrtha and Basava, out of which the majority of the historical sects came and to which Hindustan presents nothing analogous till a much later period."[3]

Dr. Tarachand discusses the growth of emotional cult, the Bhakti school, and after delineating the propositions put forth by different authorities, reaches the conclusion that:

"It is necessary to repeat that most of the elements in the southern schools of devotion and philosophy, taken singly, were derived from ancient systems; but the elements in their totality and in their peculiar emphasis betray a singular approximation to Muslim faith and therefore make the argument for Islamic influence probable."[4]

---

1. A Sufi poet who criticised social customs and usages and urged reformation. His religion is disputed.
2. K. M. Pannikar, *A Survey of Indian History*, Bombay, 1956, p. 132
3. Barth, *Religions of India*, cited from Dr Tarachand's *Influence of Islam on Indian Culture*, p 107
4. Dr. Tarachand, *Influence of Islam on Iudian Culture*. p. 107

In his another book, *Society and State in the Mughal Period*, Dr. Tarachand writes about the *Bhakti* school:

> "......there was the third group of mystics who employed the language of the people to preach their radical creeds. They mostly belonged to the lower castes and their movement represents the urge of the unprivileged masses to uplift themselves. Some of them were persecuted by Governments, some incurred social opprobrium, and others were not regarded as worthy of notice. But they were held in high esteem among the humbler classes who followed their simple teachings with eagerness and understanding. They laid stress upon the dignity of man, for they taught that every individual would reach the highest goal of human life by his own effort.................The movement arose in the fifteenth century and continued till the middle of the seventeenth, but then it declined and gradually lost its momentum.

> "The leaders of this group hailed from all parts of India but their teachings manifest a distinct influence of Islam on their beliefs."[1]

Sikhism

The same is true of Sikhism which has made an important contribution to the cultural, religious and political life of India. The system of Gurū Nānak and his followers as well as its literature and traditions, show that it owes its origin to reformation of Hinduism under Islamic influence. Its founder, Gurū Nānak, was deeply attracted by Islamic teachings. He learnt Persian and *sufi* doctrines from Syed Hasan Shāh who was reported to be deeply attached to him. He is also reported to have been closely associated with six other Muslim mystics of his time. He is stated to have performed Hajj and spent

---

1. Dr Tarachand, *Society and State in the Mughal Period*, (Delhi—1961), p. 91

some of his time in Baghdad. The most significant associate which Gurū Nānak found was, undoubtedly, Shaikh Farīd whose 142 stanzas were admitted in the *Adi Granth* itself.

Gurū Nānak called upon his followers to worship *Alakh Niranjan*—the True, the Immortal, the Self-existent, the Invisible, the Pure One God, to treat all human beings as equals and to renounce idols and incarnations. It is not only with respect to the idea of the unity of God that the identity of his teachings is discernible; he liberally made use of *sufi* teachnical terms and imagery.[1]

Tauhid and the Christian World

The impact of Islam on the Christian world has been delineated by an Egyptian scholar Dr. Ahmad Amin in the *Zuhal Islām*. He writes :

> "Several dissensions arose in Christendom which unmistakably reveal the influence of Islam. In the eighth century A. D., that is, the second and third century A. H., a movement emerged in Septmania[2] which denied confession of sin before Church authorities. It propagated the view that the bishops had no authority to absolve anyone from sin, for which one should only beseech God. Islam had no organised church nor there was any concept of such a confession of sin.

> "Another movement of a similar nature was against the presence of images and statues in churches which was known as Iconoclast. This was a sect in the eighth century A. D. or the third and fourth century A. H., which was opposed to the worship paid to statues. The Roman emperor Leo III issued an edict in 726 A. D. against showing respect to the images and statues and then interdicted it in 730 A. D. The Popes, Gregory II

---

1. See Thomas Patric Huges, *A Dictionary of Islam;* Macauliffe, *The Sikh Religion;* Sevaram Singh, *Life of Guru Nanak.*
2 A province of ancient France in its south-western part by the side of Mediterranean Sea.

and III and Jerome, the Patriarch of Constantinople, were in favour of paying homage to images and statues while Constantine V and Leo IV were opposed to it. The struggle that ensued between them need not be described here, but what we would like to emphasise is that the Iconoclast movement, as the historians acknowledge, came into existence through the impact of Islam on Christianity. They are on record that Clodius, the Pontiff of Touraine[1] (who became Pontiff in 828/213), used to destroy images and the Cross and prohibited divine honours being paid to them. He was born and brought up in Spain where he must have learnt to hate images and statues as objects of worship. Bukhārī and Muslim include a report from Ayesha, the Prophet's wife, which says: "The Prophet returned from a journey when I had hung a curtain having a few pictures on a window. When the Prophet saw it, he tore it apart and remonstrated me saying; Ayesha, the Day of Reckoning will be the hardest for those who copy God's creation."

"She further relates that she made pillows out of that cloth.[2]"

"There have been sects in Christianity which explained Trinity as belief in One God[3] and denied divinity of Jesus.[4]"

Historians of Europe, particularly those of Church, discern the influence of Islam in the conflict between the Papists and the Protestant reformers. The sixteenth Century movement for reform of abuses in Roman Church led by Martin Luther betrays the influence of Islam.[5]

The simple faith in the Unity of God had been a standing reproach to the inexplicable intricacy of Trinity. Michael

1. A former province in Western France.
2. *Shahih Bukhārī*
3. See Haine's, *Christianity and Islam in Spain*, p. 116
4. Ahmad Amin, *Zuhal Islam*, Vol. I, pp 364—65
5. See the Article on Martin Luther in the *Encyclopaedia Britannica* (1927)

Servetus (1511-1553) a contemporary of Calvin and Luther depicts his anguish in *The Errors of Trinity*:

> "How much this tradition of Trinity has alas, alas! been laughing stock of Mohammedons only God knows. The Jews also shrink from giving adherence to this fancy of ours, and laugh at our foolishness about the Trinity, and on account of its blasphemies, they do not believe that this is the Messiah promised in their Law. And not only the Mohammedons and the Hebrews, but the very beasts of the field, would make fun of us, did they grasp our fantastic notion, for all the workers of the Lord bless the One God.[1]"

Christianity amalgamated antagonistic doctrines, according to Ernest De Bunsen, framed by St. Paul which came to be recognised as the foundation of orthodox Christianity.[2] Several others like George Bernard Shaw, H. G. Wells and Dr. Albert Schweitzer have also reached the conclusion that the Pauline heresy became the foundation of Christian orthodoxy while the legitimate teachings of Jesus Christ were disowned as heretical.[3]

Luther spearheaded Protestantism which revolted against the assumption of supremacy in spiritual matters by the Roman Catholic Church and taught that man is responsible to God and not to the Church.

The Reason for Failure

A well-grounded fact demonstrated by history of religions and in tune with human psychology is that reformative or even revolutionary movements that take shape within the bosom of any religion are ultimately absorbed within that religion if they do not reject its basic postulates and maintain an ambivalent

1. Cited from Parke, D. B., *The Epic of Unitarianism*, 1957, p. 6
2. See Ernest De Bunsen, *Islam or True Christianity*, London, 1889
3. George Bernard Shaw: Preface, *Androcles and the Lion*, 1912; Albert Schweitzer, *The Mysticism of Paul and the Apostles*, 1953.

attitude towards it. The fate of all such movements, no matter to which religion they belong is the same; they lose both their identity and the message.

Reformative movements within Christianity and the Hindu sects calling the people to accept Divine Unity and brotherhood of mankind were ultimately assimilated within the religions they tried to reform. Contrary to such reformism, the prophets of God were always candid and straightforward in their condemnation of what they did not think to be correct. This is best illustrated by what Prophet Abraham is reported to have said to his people.

> "Surely an excellent pattern you have in Abraham and those who followed him. They said to their people: we disown you and what you worship beside Allah. We renounce you: enmity and hate shall reign between us until you believe in Allah alone except the saying of Abraham to his father: I shall implore Allah to forgive you, although I have no power for you with Allah at all. O Lord, in Thee we put our trust and to Thee we turn and to Thee we shall come at last."[1]

The stand taken by Prophet Abraham was meant not for the people of his time alone. He enjoined his posterity to follow his example.

> "And (recall) when Abraham said to his father and his people: I renounce what you worship save Him, who has created me and then He would guide me. And Abraham made it an abiding precept among his descendants, so that they might turn (to none but Allah)."[2]

It was this teaching which has helped Islam to maintain its pristine purity to this day. The principle to be followed for ever was : *whosoever perished might perish by a clear sign, and by a clear sign he might live who remained alive.*[3]

1. Q. 60 : 4
2. Q. 43 : 26-28
3. Q. 8 : 42

3

Concept of Human Unity and Equality

Historic Declaration of Man's Brotherhood

The second great favour conferred by the Messenger of God on human beings was the concept of equality and brotherhood of mankind. The world before him was divided by manifold divisions of castes and creeds, tribes and nations; some claiming the ranks of nobility for themselves and condemning others to the position of serfs and chattels.

These differences were by no means less sharp than those existing between the free-born and the slaves or between the worshipper and the worshipped. It was for the first time, amidst the gloom overshadowing the world for centuries, that the world heard the clarion call of human equality from the Prophet of Islam.

> "O Mankind, Your God is One and you have but one father. You are all progeny of Adam, and Adam was made of clay. Lo! the noblest among you, in the sight of God, is one who is best in conduct. No Arab has any preference over a non-Arab nor a non-Arab over an Arab save by his piety."[1]

His anouncement was in fact a twin declaration of Unity of

---

1. *Kinz-ul-'Ammāl.*

God and Unity of mankind. These are the two natural foundations for raising the edifice of peace and progress, friendship and co-operation between different peoples and nations. It created a twin relationship between human beings—that of One Lord of all mankind and the other of one father of all of them. Oneness of God was the spiritual principle of human equality just as a common lineage placed them on the same plane of humanity.

> "Mankind. fear your Lord, who created you of a single soul, and from it created its mate, and from the pair of them scattered abroad many men and women : and fear God by whom you demand one another, and the wombs, surely God ever watches over you."[1]

> "O mankind, We have created you male and female, and made you races and tribes, that you may know one another. Surely the noblest among you in the sight of God is the most God-fearing of you. God is All-knowing, All-aware.[2]"

The Prophet of Islam simultaneously announced :

> "God has put an end to the convention of pagan past taking pride in your fathers ; now there will be pious believers or unbelieving wrongdoers. All are sons of Adam and Adam was made of clay. No Arab excels a non-Arab but by his piety.[3]"

These were the teachings which made Islam, consisting of widely different tribes, races and nations, a commonwealth of the believers hailing from many countries and regions. It conferred no privileges at all : no Bani Lavis and Brahmins of Judaism and Hinduism. No tribe or race could claim any preference over another nor any blood or lineage could lay a claim to nobility for its own sake. The only criterion recognised for preference over others was an individual's endeavour to improve his morals and character. *Musnad* of Imām Ahmad

---

1. Q. 4 : 1
2. Q. 49 : 13
3. *Tirmidhi.*

reports the Prophet as saying: "Iranians would attain knowledge even if it were to be found in Venus."

Arabs have always showed highest marks of respect to those non-Arab scholars who have excelled them in religious disciplines and taken them as their teachers and guides. Strange though it may seem, they have not conferred such titles of honour on Arabs as they have on certain non-Arabs. Imām Muhammad bin Ismail-al-Bukhārī (d. 256 A. H.) was called by them as *Amir-ul-Mūminīn fil Hadīth* (Commander of the faithful in hadīth) and his *Al-Jamī'-al-Sahih* was regarded as the most authentic book next only to the Qur'ān. Imām Abul Ma'alī 'Abdul Malik al-Juwaini of Nishāpūr (d. 268 A. H.) was known as *Imām-ul-Haramayn* (Leader of the two sacred cities) and Imām Abū Hāmid Muhammad b. Muhammad al-Ghazzālī (d. 505 A. H.) as *Hujjat-ul-Islam* (Proof of Islam).

By the end of the first century of Islamic era non-Arabs had attained distinction in almost every branch of learning and attained prominence even in such sciences as *fiqh* (jurisprudence) and *Hadīth* (Traditions). Any work on literary history of the Arabs or biographies will bear witness to this development. All this happened in the golden era of Islam when the Arabs held political power in their hands.

An eminent Arab scholar 'Abdul Rahmān b. Khaldūn (d. 808 A. H.) expresses surprise over it. He says:

> "It is a strange historical fact that most of the scholars of religious and intellectual sciences were non-Arabs. The contribution of the Arabs was extremely meagre although it was an Arab civilization and its founder was also an Arab. Saibūyah held the most prominent position in Arabic Syntax, then it was Bū 'Alī Fārsī and then Az-Zajāj, and all these were non-Arabs. Same is the case with the experts in the field of *hadīth* (Traditions) *usūl fiqh* (principles of jurisprudence) and *ilm Kalām* (theological dialectics).[1]"

---

1. *Muqaddamah Ibn Khaldun*, Matb'a Bahiya, Egypt, p. 404

The announcement made by the Prophet of Islam, cited in the beginning, was made on the historic occasion of his last Hajj. When this announcement was made, perhaps, it would have been difficult for the world to fully appreciate its practical significance. It was a revolutionary call signifying release of man from the current pressures of society, its values, standards, traditions and practices.

Man always accepts any change gradually and indirectly. We can touch a covered electric wire but not a nacked one since it would give a shock which may even cause our death. And, this declaration was then more appalling than an electric shock.

The long journey of knowledge, thought and culture has now made this revolutionary call so acceptable to us that today every political and social organization swears by the Charter of Human Rights adopted by the United Nations. Now nobody is taken aback by it, but was it the same when the Prophet proclaimed it ?

Humanity before Islam

There was a time when superiority of blood and clan was accepted as a matter of fact. There are still people who trace the descent of their forefathers from the sun or the moon.

The Quran quotes the belief then held by the Jews and Christian in these words : "The Jews and the Christians say : We are the children of God, His loved ones.[1]" The Pharaohs of Egypt claimed themselves to be incarnation of *Ra*, the Sun-god, while India had several ruling families who arrogated themselves as the progeny of the sun (*suryavansi*) or the moon (*chandravarsi*,). The emperors of Iran called themselves *Kesra* or Chosroes which meant that Divine blood flowed in their veins. Chosroes II (Khosrau Parvez) had levished himself with this grandiose title : "The Immortal soul among the gods and peerless God among human beings ; glorious is whose name ;

____

1. Q. 5 : 18

dawning with the sun-rise and light of the dark-eyed night."[1]

The Caesars of Rome were called 'Augustus' which meant majestic, venerable, since they were entitled to receive divine honours.[2] The Chinese rulers deemed themselves to be the sons of Heavens. They believed that the Heaven was their God, who, with his spouse, the goddess earth, had given birth to the human beings and *Pau Ku*, the Chinese Emperor, was the first-born son of Heaven enjoying supernatural powers.[3] The Arabs were so proud of their language that every nation besides their own was an *'ajami* or dumb to them. Likewise, the Quraysh of Mecca being conscious of maintaining their superiority claimed a privileged position even during the Hajj. They never went to the plain of 'Arafat with others. They stayed in the Mosque at Mecca or went to Muzdalifa claiming that privilege on the ground that they belonged to the House of God. They also claimed themselves to be the elites of Arabia.[4]

The most glaring peculiarity of the religio-social structure of India of the olden days was the all-powerful caste system. This rigid social order having the sanction of religion behind it allowed no inter-mixing of races for it was meant to protect the privileged position of Brahmins. It classified the population of India into four classes with reference to the vocation followed by a particular family in which an individual was born. The system which covered the whole gamut of social life in India divided the people into four castes, namely, (i) the *Brahmin* or the learned and priestly class, (ii) the *Kshattriyas* or the fighting and ruling class, (iii) The *Vaisyas* or trading and agricultural people, and (iv) the *Sudras* or the lowest caste, created from the foot of God, in order to serve the above three classes.

This law of caste distinctions gave to the Brahmin the

1. A. Christensen, *L' Iran Sous Les Sassanides*, Paris, 1944 (Urdu translation by Prof. Mohd. Iqbal, *Iran ba 'ahd-i-Sasāniyān*), p. 64
2. Victor Chopart, *The Roman World*, London, 1928, p. 418
3. James Carcarn, *History of China.*
4. *Bukhārī*, on the authority of 'Āyesha.

distinction, superiority and sanctity not enjoyed by any other caste. He was sinless and the saved even if he destroyed the three worlds ; no impost could be levied on him ; he could not be punished for any crime ; while the *Sudra* could not accumulate wealth or touch a *Brahmin* or a sacred scripture.[1]

The *Vaisyas*, or the working classes like weavers, boatmen, butchers etc., and the *Sudras* like scavengers were not allowed to live in a city. They came into the town after the daybreak and left it before the sun-set. Not allowed to enjoy the amenities of urban life, they lived in the rural slums.[2]

The most precious gift that Muslims brought to India was the concept of human equality which was completely unknown to India. The Muslim society was not divided into castes and no trade was allocated to any particular class. The Muslims mixed freely, lived and dined together, all were free to read or write and carry on any occupation. The Muslim social order posed a challenge to that obtaining in India, but it also proved a blessing for it. The rigour of caste distinction was weakened and movements of social reform were able to concentrate on the shortcomings of Hindu society and consequently untouchability was removed to a large extent.

Jawahar Lal Nehru, the ex-Prime Minister of India, has acknowledged the debt India owes to Islam. He writes in the *Discovery of India* :

> ' The impact of the invaders from the north-west and of Islam on India had been considerable. It had pointed out and shown up the abuses that had crept into Hindu society—the patrification of caste, untouchability, exclusiveness carried to fantanstic lengths. The idea of the brotherhood of Islam and of the theoretical equality of its adherents made a powerful appeal, especially to those in the Hindu fold who were denied any semblance of equal treatment.[3]"

1. For detailed information see *Manu Smirti*, Chap, 1, 2, 8-11.
2. *Ibid*.
3. Jawahar Lal Nehru, *The Discovery of India*, Calcutta, 1946, p. 225.

Impact of Islam on Hinduism can be seen in the move-
ment of *Bhakti* (love and devotion) which began in South
India during Muslim rule and spread to the whole country.
Describing this movement Dr. Tara Chand writes:

> "...... along with them marched a goodly company of
> saintly men who addressed themselves to the comm-
> on people. They spoke the common people's dialects
> and in the main imparted their message through
> word of mouth. Many of them were endowed with
> the gift of poetry and their homely memorable verse
> went direct into the heart of their listeners. Their
> avoidance of the learned jargon, their simple teachings
> stressing the love of God and of man, their denunciation
> of idolatry and caste, of hypocrisy, inequality and
> the externalia of religion, their sincerity, purity and
> dedicated life appealed to wide circles among the
> masses.
>
> "Their utterances gave shape to the modern Indian
> languages. Their enthusiasm stirred the springs of
> life and moved men to high endeavour and unselfish
> behaviour. There is a strange exaltation in society in
> every region during the fifteenth, sixteenth and seven-
> teenth centuries, which cannot be accounted for with-
> out taking into consideration this sudden outburst of
> spiritual energy. These centuries are filled with
> voices—at once warning and encouraging—of truly
> noble and large-hearted men in surprisingly large
> numbers. Yet most of them were of humble origin
> and they destroyed the myth of aristocracy based on
> birth.[1]"

The spirit of human brotherhood built up by Islam is not
hampered by concepts of racialism or sectarianism, be it
linguistic, historic, traditionalistic or even of dogmatic nature.

---

1. Dr. Tara Chand, *Society and State in the Mughal Period,* Publications
   Division, Ministry of Information and Broadcasting, 1961, pp. 88-89.

Its power to unite different races and nations in one brotherhood has always been recognised. A noted orientalist H. A.
R. Gibb says :

> "But Islam has yet a further service to render to the cause
> of humanity . . . . . No other society has such a record of
> success in uniting in an equality of status, of opportu-
> nity and of endeavour so many and so various races of
> mankind. The great Muslim communities of Africa.
> India, and Indonesia, perhaps also the small Muslim
> community of Japan, show that Islam has still the
> power to reconcile apparently irreconcilable elements
> of race and tradition. If ever the opposition of the
> great societies of the East and West is to be replaced
> by co-operation, the mediation of Islam is an indis-
> pensable condition.[1]"

The British historian A. J. Toyanbee agrees with Gibb that
Islam alone can efface race consciousness.

> "The extinction of race consciousness as between Muslims
> is one of the outstanding achievements of Islam, and
> in the contemporary world there is, as it happens, a
> crying need for the propagation of this Islamic virtue
> . . . . "

> "Though in certain other respects the triumph of the
> English-speaking peoples may be judged, in retrospect,
> to have been a blessing to mankind, in this perilous
> matter of race feeling it can hardly be denied that it
> has been a misfortune."[2]

Islam was the first religion which preached and practised
democracy. The well-known Indian freedom fighter and poetess
Mrs. Sarojini Naidu witnessed and affirmed this quality of
Islam.

> "It was the first religion that preached and practised
> democracy ; for, in the mosque when the call from the

---

1. H. A. R. Gibb, *Whither Islam ?* London, 1932, p. 379
2. A. J. Toyanbee, *Civilization on Trial*, New York, 1948, p. 205.

> Minaret is sounded and the worshippers are gathered together, the democracy of Islam is embodied five times a day when the peasant and the king kneel side by side and proclaim, "God alone is great." I have been struck over and over again by this indivisible unity of Islam that makes a man distinctly a brother. When you meet an Egyptian, an Algerian, an Indian and a Turk in London, what matters that Egypt was the motherland of one and India the motherland of another." [1]

Malcolm X was a racist for whom 'devil white man' was a Satan. He shed all his prejudices on coming in contact with the Muslims. He recounts his own experience :

> "During the past eleven days here in the Muslim World, I have eaten from the same plate, drunk from the same glass, and slept in the same bed (or on the same rug) — while praying to the *same* God — with fellow Muslims, whose eyes were bluest of the blue, whose hair was blondest of the blond, and whose skin was the whitest of the white. And in the *words* and in the *actions* and in the *deeds* of the 'white' Muslims, I felt the same sincerity that I felt among the black African Muslims of Nigeria, Sudan, and Ghana.
>
> "We were truly all the *same* (brothers) — because their belief in one God had removed the 'white' from their *minds*, the 'white' from their *behaviour*, and the 'white' from their *attitude*.
>
> "I could see from this, that perhaps if white Americans could accept the Oneness of God, then perhaps, too, they could accept *in reality* the Oneness of Man — and cease to measure, and hinder, and harm others in terms of their 'differences' in color." [2]

1. The Ideals of Islam in *Speeches and Writings of Sarojini Naidu*, Madras, 1918. p. 169.

2. *The Autobiography of Malcolm X* (ed. Alex Haley) Essex, 1965, pp. 419—20.

4

Proclamation of Human Dignity

The third universal gift of Islam is its declaration that man has been endowed with the highest rank and dignity in the entire scheme of God's creation. Before the prophethood of Muhammad, on whom be peace and blessings of God, man had degraded himself to the position of the most inconsequential being on earth. Numerous beasts and trees connected with mythological traditions and pagan beliefs were held as holy and cared for more than man himself. They had to be protected even at the cost of innocent lives; sometimes human beings were sacrificed at the alter of these holy objects. We still come across such gory incidents even in such civilized countries as India.

Prophet Muhammad (peace be upon him) restored the dignity of man by declaring that man is the most respectable and prized being in the whole Universe and nothing has a greater claim to honour and love and protection than he. The holy Prophet raised man to the highest conceivable level, that is, the position of the vicegerent of God on earth. It was for man that the world was created. Says the Qurān :

"It is He who created for you all that is". [1]

The Qurān described man as the paramount and best of

___

1. Q. 2:29.

creations in the whole Universe.

> "We have honoured the children of Adam and guided
> them by land and sea,
> And provided them with good things and exalted them
> above many of Our creations." [1]

What can affirm human eminence and honour better than this observation by the Prophet of Islam.

> "The entire creation constitutes the family of God and he
> is dearest to Him who is the best in his dealings with
> God's family. [2]"

Another *Hadith* related by Abū Huraira from the holy Prophet, throws light on the nobility of human existence and also alludes to man's ability to achieve divine propinquity through service to mankind by a meaningful allegory :

> "Allah will ask on the Day of Judgment : 'O Children of
> Adam, I fell ill but you did not come to see Me ?'
> Man will say in reply, 'Allah ! Thou wert the Lord
> of the worlds ! how could have I attended Thee ?'
> God will then say, 'Did you not know one of my
> servants had fallen ill, but you did not come to attend
> him. Did you not know that if you had attended him,
> you would have found Me by his side ?'

> 'O Children of Adam, I asked for food from you, but you
> did not give it to Me,' God will ask. Man will answer,
> 'Allah ! Thou wert the Sustainer of the worlds ! how
> could have I fed Thee ?' God will then say, 'One of
> my servants asked you for food, but you refused it to
> him. Had you fed him, you would have found Me
> near him. !'

> 'O Children of Adam, I asked for water from you, but you
> refused it to Me,' God will ask. Man will again say
> in reply, 'Thou wert the Lord of the worlds, How
> could have I quenched Thy thirst ?' God will answer,

1. Q. 17 : 70.
2. *Sunan Baihaqi.*

> 'One of My servants demanded water from you but
> you refused. Had you given him water you would
> have found Me near him. !" [1]

Can there be a better concept of human dignity and
nobility ? Has man ever been granted this honour under any
religion or social philosophy ?

The Prophet of Islam has made divine mercy contingent on
being kind to man.

> "The Most Merciful is compassionate to the softhearted.
> Show mercy to those on the earth and the Owner of
> Heavens will be merciful to you." [2]

All those who know about the social and political condition
of the world prior to the advent of Islam can easily appreciate
the determined effort holy Prophet had to make in order to
drive home the concept of worth and dignity of man.

Lives of innumerable human beings depended on the whims
of a single individual before the prophethood of Muhammad
(peace be upon him). Any tyrant could wade in blood across
countries and continents for gaining political ascendancy or just
for satisfying his whims.

Alexander the Great (356-324 B. C.) rose like a tempest,
subdued Syria and Egypt, and crossing the Babylonia and Turkis-
tan reached India. He swept the older civilizations before him.
Julius Caesar (102-44 B. C.) and several other conquerors like
Hannibal (247-182 B. C.) exterminated large populations remor-
selessly as if those were not human beings but beasts of prey. [3]

These pitiless massacres continued all over the world even
after the advent of Jesus Christ. The Roman Emperor Nero
(A. D. 54-68) murdered his own wife and mother, persecuted
his own countrymen and played with the fiddle while the Rome
burnt, for which he was probably himself responsible. [4]

1. *Sahih Muslim.*
2. *Sunan Abī Dawūd.*
3. See William L. Langer, *Encyclopaedia of World History*, 1964.
4. *Ibid.*

Barbarians like Goths and Vandals were busy destroying civilisation in Europe and Africa only a hundred years before the prophethood of Muhammad (peace be upon him).[1]

Little regard for human life among the Arabs had made fights and forays a pastime for them and even the most trivial matter could lead them to the battle-field. Bakr and Taghlab, the two tribes of Bani Wā'il, continued to fight for forty years during which they fought many a sanguinary battle although it all started by the shooting of an arrow at the udder of a camel which mixed the milk with blood. Jassās b. Marrah killed Kalayb and then Bakr and Taghlab started fighting about which Kalayb's brother Al-Muhalhil remarked; "Men have died, mothers have become childless, children have become orphans; tears stream from the eyes and the dead are lying shroudless."

Similarly the battle of Dāhis-o-Ghabra was sparked off simply because Dāhis, the horse of Qays b. Zuhair, had overtaken that of Hudaiqa b. Badr. A man of Asad slapped Qays at the instance of Hudaiqa which made his horse lose the race. Thereafter the war of attrition started in which a large number of people lost their lives and many had to leave their hearths and homes.[2]

The number of battles fought by the holy Prophet was twenty-seven or twenty-eight while he is reported to have sent out sixty forays and expeditions. In all these battles and expeditions only 1018 persons, Muslims as well as non-Muslims, lost their lives.

The purpose of these fightings was to restore law and order and protect human life and property from its senseless destruction. A civilised code of conduct was prescribed for the warfare which changed the character of war from persecution to disciplinary action.[3]

1. See William Langer, *Encyclopaedia of World History.*
2. *Ayyam-ul-'Arab.*
3. The Prophet gave detailed instructions to the troops sent by him not to indulge in any act of cruelty. 'The Expeditions at a Glance' in the author's *Muhammed Rasūlullāh* (pp. 361-64) can be seen in this connection.

The moral teachings of Islam create such a strong sense of human diginity that one never treats another man as a sub-human being. He never treats another man as a chattel or slave nor discriminates between himself and others which is very often the cause of degrading others. An incident preserved by history amply illustrates the sense of human dignity embeded by Islam. Anas relates that he was with 'Umar, the second Caliph, when an Egyptian Copt complained to the Caliph that his horse had beaten that of Muhammad son of 'Amr b. al-'Ās, the Governor of Egypt, which was witnessed by a number of persons. When he claimed that he had won the race, Muhammad got enraged and lashed him with a whip. Caliph 'Umar asked him to wait and wrote to 'Amr b. al-'As asking him and his son to present themselves before him. 'Amr b. al-'Ās sent for his son and enquired about the matter who denied having committed any crime. Then both 'Amr b. al-'Ās and his son repaired to Madina. Caliph 'Umar sent for the Copt and giving him a whip asked him to beat the son of 'Amr b. al-'Ās. After the Copt had exacted retribution, Caliph 'Umar ordered the Copt to move the whip over the head of 'Amr b. al-'Ās for it was because of him that he had been flogged. The Copt refused saying that he had already had his revenge. Thereupon 'Umar remarked : "Had you beaten him I would not have intervened." Then, turning to 'Amr b. al-'Ās he said, "Whence did you make them slaves who had been born free ?" Thereafter turning to the Copt, 'Umar said, "Go back and have no fear. If anything happens, inform me."[1]

---

1. Ibn Jawzi, *Sirat 'Umar Ibn al-Khattāb*, pp. 86-87.

5

Raising the position of Women and Restoration of their rights

Women before Islam

A few introductory remarks would be necessary for appreciating the measures taken by Islam for ameliorating the condition of women. I would better give a few extracts from *Al-Mar'ato fil-Qurān* by the learned Arab scholar 'Abbās Mahmūd al-'Aqqād who has made an in-depth study of the subject.

Describing the position of women under pre-Islamic religions and societies, he writes :

"The Laws of Manu[1] accorded no personality to

1. Manu is regarded as the framer of the code of Hindu religious and social Laws. He appears to have been a primitive mythological personage, whose time and character cannot be determined with any certainity. In the *Vedas* he is described as a god, but the writings attributed to him present him as the ancestor and legislator of human race. This position is, however, claimed for certain other characters as well in the ancient scriptures.

   Manu Smirti expounds the ancient code of religious and social legislation, although it is attributed also to Go Maharaj, taken as the spiritual successor of Manu. Nevertheless, it is the oldest tract of Hindu religious and social laws, dating in its present form from about the third century A. D. (Extracted from the writings of Ganga Nath Jha and Dr. Jaiswal who are considered authorities on the history of Hindu Law).

woman save that as a dependent of her father or husband and in the event of the death of both, as a client of her son. On the death of all the three she had to content herself as a hanger-on of one of the near relations of her husband. She could never become self-dependent. The injustice to which she was subjected, even more than in her economic affairs, was in the case of her separation from her husband ; for, she was required to die with her dead husband on the funeral pyre. This was an age-old custom followed from the ancient days of Brahmanic civilisation to the seventeenth century when it was given up owing to rising public opinion against it.

"The code of Hammurabi[1] treated woman as a pet. The status of woman under this code is illustrated by one of its provisions which said that if a man killed the daughter of another man, he had to hand over his own daughter to the aggrieved person who might kill her in retribution, keep her as a slave-girl or reprieve the punishment, but she was more often slain to meet the demand of the law.

"In ancient Greece woman neither enjoyed any freedom nor had any right. She was made to live in big houses away from the main thoroughfares, having few windows and a guard posted at the door. With little attention paid to the housewives and mistresses, soirees with dancing-girls and women of easy virtue had become a common pastime. Women were not allowed to join men in social gatherings : they never joined the study circles of the philosophers. Harlots, divorced women and courtesan slave-girls enjoyed a greater title to fame and respect than the married women.

"Aristotle censured Spartans for being kind to their womenfolk and giving them right of inheritance, divorce

---

1. The Babylonian King, author of famous code of laws, and unifier of the Babylonian Empire (c. 2360 B. C.).

and self-dependence and considered these as the reasons for the downfall of Sparta.

"The Romans of the old treated woman much like the same as the ancient Hindus for she was to remain under the wardship of her father, husband or the son. During the bloom of their cultural glory they held the view that neither a woman could be unshackled nor her neck could be freed as the saying by Cato[1] goes : *Nanguam exvitur servitus mulie Brio.* The Roman woman got freedom from the restrictions imposed on her only after the Roman slaves wrested their freedom through insurrection".

After describing the status of women in the ancient Egypt. Mahmūd 'Aqqād says :

"Egyptian civilization and its social laws had already run its course before the advent of Islam. With the downfall of Roman civilization in the Middle East and as a reaction to its luxuriousness and dissipation a strong trend disdaining the worldly life had set in Egypt. The life itself and the association with one's kith and kin had lost attraction while a general inclination towards monasticism had made the flesh and women appear as sinful.

"This tenor of the Middle Ages had so undermined the position of women that the ecclesiastics continued to discuss the nature of women in all seriousness up to the fifteenth century. The questions whether woman had a soul or was a body without soul and whether she was eligible to salvation or doomed to damnation were vigorously debated in the synod of Macon.[2] The majority view was that she did not possess the soul fit for salvation, the only exception being the Virgin Mary, mother of Jesus Christ.

1. Marcus Porcius Cato (234–149 B.C.) became in succession censor, aedile, praetor and consul, subjugated Spain, and disliked and denounced all innovations.
2. A town of France on the Saone.

"This tendency of the later Roman period was responsible for the degradation of women in the subsequent phase of Egyptian civilization. Actually, the barbarism of the Romans was responsible for giving rise to monasticism and other-worldliness in Egyptian society. A large number of people came to regard the secluded life under religious vows dedicated to prayer, contemplation and development of spiritual faculties as a means to attaining nearness to God and saving themselves from the machinations of the Devil (of which women was the greatest inducement).

"A number of Western orientalists contend that the Islamic *Shari'ah* is based on the Hebrew Law but this view is confuted by a comparison of the status enjoyed by the women under the Pentateuch and the Qur'ān. A daughter had no right to inheritance, under the Pentateuch, from her father if the deceased had a male child.

"It was an obligation regulating the gifts that the property owned by anyone should not pass on to another family on his death.

"The Jewish Laws relating to inheritance provided that so long as there was a male child of a desceased person, his daughter would not be entitled to inheritance, and the daughter inheriting from the deseased father would not be allowed to marry into another tribe. Similarly, she could not transfer the inherited property to another tribe. This law has been repeated at several places in the Torah.

"Now we turn to the country where the Quranic teachings first came to be preached. One should not expect that the women were treated more favourably in the ancient Arabia. In fact, the treatment meted out to her in the Arabian peninsula was worse than in any other country of the world. If she enjoyed any respect in a particular case, it was because she

happened to be the daughter of the chief of a powerful tribe or the mother of an illustrious son. She was
thus not entitled to any respect or honour by virtue
of belonging to the fair sex. She was no doubt
protected by the father, husband, brother or son but
like any other material possession of a man. It was
against the tribal sentiment of honour that anybody
should lay his hands on anything under the protection
of another man and this included one's horses, herds,
wells and pastures. The women were likewise inherited by the heirs of the deseased person like his
property. Woman in Arabia enjoyed no social status,
rather, the shame attached to her made the father
bury alive his own daughter. The moneys spent on
the upkeep of the daughter was deemed as a burden
although a Bedouin was not miser in spending on his
goods and chattels or a slave-girl. Even those who
allowed their daughters to remain alive considered her
no more than an exchangeable good which could be
inherited by the deceased's heir or sold or pawned for
payment of a loan or interest. She was spared
these humiliations only if she belonged to a powerful
tribe prepared to extend its protection to her."[1]

Buddhism

Nor did Buddhism, inspite of its universalism, place women
on an equal level with men. Its highest morality demanded
entire abstinence from them. Dorner quotes *Chullavagga*[2] to
illustrate the position of women in Buddhism in these words :

> "Inscrutable as the way of a fish in water is the nature of
> women, those thieves of many devices, with whom
> truth is hard to find."[3]

---

1. 'Abbās Mahmūd al-'Aqqād, *Al-Mar'ato fil Qur'ān*, Dār-ul-Hilāl,
   Egypt, n. d., pp. 51-57.
2. *c. f.* Oldenburg, *Buddha*, 1906, pp. 169f. and 355f.
3 *Encyclopedia of Religion and Ethics*, Edinburg, 1921, Vol. V, p. 271.

Hinduism

The position of women in Hinduism as described by the same writer reads :

> "In *Brahmanism*, again, marriage is made much of: every one ought to marry. Still, according to the *Laws of Manu*, the husband is the head of the wife; she must do nothing to displease him, even if he give himself to other loves; and, should he die, she must never utter the name of another man. If she marry again, she is excluded from the heaven where her first husband dwells. Unfaithfulness on the wife's part is punished with the utmost rigour. 'A women is never independent'. She cannot inherit, and after her husband's death she is subject to their eldest son. The husband may even chastise her with the bamboo-rod."[1]

Mrs. Ray Strachey writing about the 'Women: Her Status and its influence on History' paints a similar picture of women's condition under Hinduism.

She says :

> "The *Rig-Veda*, which includes the collected legends of Manu, the ancestor of mankind, assigns to women a low and miserable place, and from that date onwards they have had no 'status' at all. For it came to be thought that they were spiritually negligible, all but soulless, unable to survive after death without the virtue of man. With their faith to kill their hopes, and with all the imprisoning customs which gradually sprang from it, it was impossible that eastern women should produce any great outstanding figure.

> "When creating them, Manu allotted to women a love of their bed, of their seat and of ornament, impure desires, wrath, dishonesty and bad conduct......women are as impure as falsehood itself, that is the fixed rule

---

Encyclopedia of Religion and Ethics, Edinburg, 1921, Vol. V, p. 271.

.... It is the nature of women to reduce men in this world, and for that reason the wise are never unguarded in the company of females......a woman is never fit for independence.

"This, with much more to the same effect in the teaching of the Hindu scriptures, and on that discouraging basis Hindu women have had to build their lives.

"The custom of child marriage, of widow hatred, of 'sati' and of the 'purdah' seem almost natural in a society in which women's only importance lay in the bearing of sons. Perhaps the exposure of the female infants was, after all, a kindness in a world where women were believed to be 'a great whirlpool of suspicion, a dwelling place of vices, full of deceits, a hinderance in the way of heaven, and the gate of hell.''[1]

China

The same writer describes the position of women in China in these words.

"Further east, in China, things were no better, and the custom of crippling the feet of little girls, which was intended to keep them helpless and ladylike, reveals the attitude of the Chinese. If applied, of course, only to the high born and wealthy, but it was a true symbol of the condition of all the women in the Celestial Empire.''[2]

Christendom

The attitude of the Christian world towards women was until recently determined by the teachings of the Bible: 'Unto the women he said,......and thy desire shall be to thy husband, and he shall rule over thee' (Ge. 3 : 16) 'Wives, submit yourselves unto your own husbands, as unto the Lord. For the husband is the head of the wife, even as Christ is the head of the Church, and he is the saviour of the body. Therefore as

1. *Universal History of World*, (ed.) J. A. Hammerton (London) n. d..
   Vol. I, p. 378.
2. *Ibid.*

the Church is subject unto Christ, so let the wives be to their own husbands in every thing.' (Eph. 5: 22-24). The woman was condemned by the Church Fathers as the most potent source of sin and temptation. It was Eve who allegedly tempted Adam, according to the creation story of *Genesis*, to eat the forbidden fruit and thus laid the burden of Original Sin upon man. Thus some Greek orthodox monasteries to this day do not only prohibit any women from entering the premises but even female domestic animals.[1] Women's rights to inheritance, obtaining divorce, acquiring property, succession and remarriage were beyond the laws of the West until recently.

England

In regard to the status of women in England, which could be true of other countries in the West, Mrs. Ray Strachey says:
> "........ this favourite was denied every civil right, was shut out from education and from all but the lowest forms of wage earning, and surrendered her whole property on marriage."[2]

Women in Islam

Now let us compare the teachings of Islam, the status and rights it gives to woman, with her position under other religions. It will be seen how Islam has restored her rights as well as her dignity, assigned her a proper place in the society and protected her against not only the conceit of men but also from irrational and cruel customs. Even a cursory glance over the Qur'ān is enough to disclose the difference between the attitudes of Islam and the pagan past in regard to women which, in the course of things, regulate all dealings with her, both at individual and social levels.

The Quranic verses referring to the fair sex, comprising half of humanity, create a sense of self-confidence in woman.

1. Maryam Jameelah, *Islam Versus Ahl al-Kitab, Past and Present,* Lucknow, 1983, p. 298.
2. *Universal History of the World*, op. cit., Vol. I, p. 382.

They assign her a place in the society as well as in the sight of God and encourage her to make efforts for the service of religion and knowledge, cooperate in spreading goodness and virtue and build a healthy society. Wherever the Qur'ān refers to God's acceptance of good deeds, attainment of salvation and success in the hereafter, it refers to men as well as women.

> "And whosoever does deeds of righteousness, be it male or female, believing—they shall enter Paradise, and not be wronged a single date-spot."[1]

> "And then Lord answers them : "I waste not the labours of any that labours among you, be you male or female—the one of you is as the other."[2]

The Qur'ān promises 'goodly life' to men and women alike in an equal measure. This 'goodly life' means a life of peace and contentment and honour in this very world.

> "Whosoever works righteously, male or female, and is a believer, We shall assuredly give him to live in a goodly life ; and surely recompense them their wage for the best of what they have been doing."[3]

The Qur'ān's elaborate style of mentioning both men and women as equally fit for attaining every individual virtue and being equally recompensed for their good deeds, righteousness and the religious duties performed by them is designed not merely to emphasise absence of any actual difference between the two, but also meant to drive home the capability of women to attain through their goodness a grace even higher than men for the latter were perceptive to their own superiority, even denied all excellence to women, as it was then taught by all the religious philosophies and modes of thought. Now, read the following verses of the Qur'ān keeping in mind the reason behind adopting a deliberately diffused strain.

> "Lo ! men who surrender unto Allah, and women who surrender, and men who believe and women who

1. Q. 4 : 124
2. Q. 3 : 195
3. Q. 16 : 97

> believe, and men who obey and women who obey, and
> men who speak the truth and women who speak the
> truth, and men who persevere (in righteousness) and
> women who persevere, and men who are humble and
> women who are humble, and men who give alms and
> women who give alms, and men who fast and women
> who fast, and men who guard their modesty and women
> who guard their modesty, and men who remember
> Allah and women who remember—Allah hath prepared
> for them forgiveness and a vast reward."[1]

The Qur'ān does not speak of women in regard to their
goodness and devotions only, but also mentions them with men
who attain knowledge and excellence and undergo hardship in
bidding the good and forbidding the wrong. It wants men
and women to unite their efforts in restoring goodness and
righteousness.

> "And the believers, the men and the women, are friends
> one of the other, they enjoin the right and forbid the
> wrong, they establish worship and they pay the poor-
> due, and they obey Allah and His messenger. Those—
> upon them Allah will have mercy; Allah is Mighty,
> Wise".[2]

The Qur'ān promulgates a new order of nobility—it depends
not on colour or race or sex but on piety.

> "O mankind, We have created you male and female, and
> appointed you races and tribes, that you may know
> one another. Surely the noblest among you in the
> sight of Allah is the most pious of you. Verily Allah is
> Knowing, Wise."[3]

These verses were meant to inspire self-reliance, self-respect
and courage among woman or what our psychologists will regard
as intended to shed her inferiority complex.

---

1. Q. 33 : 35
2. Q. 9 : 71
3. Q. 49 : 13

The result of these teachings was that in every age from the time of the Prophet of Islam to this day we find numerous illustrious **women** who achieved eminence, as teachers, guides, fighters in the way of God and nurses in the battle-field, litterateurs, memorisers of the Qur'ān, narrators of Traditions, pious and righteous, who have been held in the highest esteem by the Muslims.[1]

Islam gave women the right to ratify or annul her marriage, the right of inheritance and to own and dispose of her property, and several other rights besides the right to participate in congregational prayers. These can be found in any treatise on Islamic jurisprudence.

Opinions of Western Scholars.

Several Western scholars and experts of sociology have acknowledged that the Quranic teachings in regard to women place them on an equal legal position with men and raise their social position in the society. We shall give here the opinions of only a few scholars of whom Mrs. Annie Besant is the first. An Irish woman, she was the founder of a reformative movement in India, headed the Theosophical Society of South India and was an active worker in the struggle for freedom of India. The opinion expressed by her is significant since a woman scholar should naturally feel more concerned about anything concerning women's rights.

She says:

> "You can find others stating that the religion (Islam) is evil because it sanctions a limited polygamy. But you do not hear as a rule the criticism which I spoke out one day in a London hall where I knew that the audience was entirely uninstructed. I pointed out to them that monogamy with a blended mass of prostitution was a hypocrisy and more degrading than a limited polygamy. Naturally a statement that gives

---

1. Several compilations listing illustrious Muslim women of different times exist which can be consulted.

offence, but has to be made, because it must be remembered that the law of Islam in relation to women was until lately, when parts of it have been imitated in England, the most just law as far as women are concerned, to be found in the world. Dealing with property, dealing with rights of succession and so on, dealing with cases of divorce, it was far beyond the law of the West, in the respect which was paid to the rights of women. These things are forgotten while people are hypnotised by the words monogamy and polygamy and do not look at what lies behind it in the West—the frightful degradation of women who are thrown into the streets when their first protectors, weary of them, no longer give them any assistance."[1]

Another scholar, N. J. Coulson, writes in *A History of Islamic Law* :

"Without doubt it is the general subject of the position of women, married women in particular, which occupies pride of place in the Quranic laws. Rules on marriage and divorce are numerous and varied, and, with their general objective of improvement of women's status, represent some of the most radical reforms of the Arabian customary law effected in the Quran.............
She is now endowed with a legal competence, she did not possess before. In the laws of divorce the supreme innovation of the Quran lies in the introduction of the 'waiting period' *(idda)*."[2]

Describing the process of emancipation of women Dorner writes in the *Encyclopedia of Religion and Ethics.*

"Certainly the Prophet raised the status of women above that assigned to them in ancient Arabia ; in particular,

---

1. Annie Besant, *The Life and Teachings of Muhammad*, Madras, 1932, p. 3
2. N. J. Coulson, *Islamic Surveys : A History of Islamic Law*, Edinburg, 1971, p. 14

the woman was no longer a mere heritable chattel of her deceased husband's estate, but was herself capable of inheriting ; while, again a free women could not now be forced into marriage, and, in cases of divorce, the husband was required to let the wife retain what he gave her at marriage. Moreover, women of upper classes might occupy themselves with poetry and science, and even act as teachers, while those of lower rank not seldom shared the joys and sorrows of their husbands, as mistresses of their household. The mother likewise must be treated with respect."[1]

Revolutionary Concept

The new concept of women's equality with men enunciated in the Quranic verses and the teachings of the Prophet was so revolutionary that it virtually meant her rebirth in a new society. In the pre-Islamic world she was everywhere regarded as a dumb and pet animal or lifeless object of inheritance : she was either buried alive or kept as an article of decoration. It was at this time that she was accorded her rightful place in the society and family life by a clean sweep brought about by Islam. The change was welcomed all over the world, particularly, in the countries where Islam made a debut triumphantly and took over the reins of government. It also played a vital role as a reformative agent in those societies where woman had no right to live by herself and was forced, to immolate herself in the event of her husband's death.

The Muslim rulers of India did all that was possible to reform the Indian society and to discourage such customs as *Sati*, but they always ensured that they did not interfere with the religion, customs and traditions of others. The French physician, Dr. Francois Bernier who visited India during the reign of Shāhjahān has described the efforts made by Muslim rulers to discourage the custom of self-immolation among

---

1. *Enyclopedia of Religion and Ethics*, Edinburg, 1912, Vol. V., p. 271

Hindu women.

> "The number of victims is less now than formerly; the Mahometans, by whom the country is governed, doing all in their power to suppress the barbarous custom. They do not, indeed, forbid it by positive law, because it is a part of their policy to leave the idolatrous population, which is so much more numerous than their own, in the free exercise of its religion; but the practice is checked by indirect means. No woman can sacrifice herself without permission from the governor of the province in which she resides, and he never grants it until he shall have ascertained that she is not to be turned aside from her purpose: to accomplish this desirable end the governor reasons with the widow and makes her enticing promises; after which, if these methods fail, he sometimes sends her among his women, that the effect of their remonstrances may be tried. Notwithstanding these obstacles, the number of self-immolations is still very considerable, particularly in the territories of the *Rajas*, where no Mahometan governors are appointed."[1]

Women in the Modern West

Feminist movement has been flaunted with such a fanfare by the modern West that one is led to believe that Europe and America should be a heaven for women where they should be leading a contented life with complete independence and self-respect. However, the reports appearing in the press and observations of Western intellectuals are sufficient to reveal that all that glitters is not gold.

Industrially developed countries of the West are currently facing a new threat—a wave of misogamy that has been termed

---

1. *Travels of the Moghul Empire by Francois Bernier (A. D. 1656-1668),* (ed.) Archibald Constable, Westminister, Vol. I, pp. 306-307

as 'Domestic Violence' by the United Nations' Centre for Social Development and Human Affairs. The Centre based at Vienna has conducted two surveys which reveal its deep concern over the fast growing rate of divorce in the West. These reports also highlight increasing domestic violence which has been described as the most unhappy and agonising development to which the Centre wants serious attention to be paid by all well-meaning persons. These reports say that it is no longer possible to overlook this new phenomenon. Concern has also been expressed over the rapid erosion of traditional values which were the props of family life and guaranteed protection and maintenance of the weaker members of the family as well as care and guidance to the children. The entire family structure in these countries is now breaking up, the couples' personal life is devoid of any spark of affection and none among the spouses has the least desire to accept any responsibility of the other. An international symposium organised by the United Nations Organization the previous year spotlighted the growing trend of violence to the wives in the developed countries, use of physical force for the satisfaction of sex and callousness shown in maintenance and guidance of the children. All these emanate from the disintegrating family life in the West.

Another colloquy on 'Violence in Society' was organised by the Ministry of Justice in Canada during October, 1985. There was a consensus among the participants in it that domestic violence had assumed the shape of a heinous offence which could no longer be ignored by the mass media. Mr. King, the Public Prosecutor of Canada, expressed the view that factors chiefly responsible for increase in this trend were alcoholism and addiction to drugs. He pleaded that the notice of these offences which destroyed peace of the home should be taken by the police much in the same way as bank robberies and that they should be made cognizable offence. The debate showed a general consensus about the fact that the situation in the United States of America was still worse where, on an average, 16 per cent couples were afflicted by this menace.

According to American social scientists, 3,76,000 minors were subjected to criminal assault and rape in a year while domestic violence very often took the shape of physical assault of the wives, tying their hands and feet and hanging them upside down, strangulating the assaulted women and using violent means for sexual satisfaction. The situation in the Soviet Russia is no better where, too, the divorce is common and family structure is fast disintegrating.

6

Infusing Hope and Confidence into Man

Another gift of Islam was giving hope and confidence to man at the time when a general sense of pessimism springing from the then prevalent notion of worthlessness of human nature and hopelessness of Divine succour filled the air. The ancient religions of the East and Middle Eastern countries as well as the Pauline Christianity had an equal share in producing this mental climate. The philosophy of re-birth preached by the religions of ancient India, which assigned no place to free will and decision of man, meant that the present life of a man was but a form of retribution to one's actions during the previous life: one's fate was sealed either as a dissolute swaggerer or a helpless victim.

Christianity proclaimed the Original Sin of man and its atonement by Jesus Christ which shook the confidence of millions, all over the world, in the amenability of their own actions and the mercy of God.

It was in this environment of complete pessimism that Muhammad (peace be upon him) affirmed that man was born with a clean slate and perfect freedom of action. Man was, declared the Prophet, the author of his actions, both good and evil, and deserved reward or punishment in accordance with his own decision that shaped the course of his actions. None was responsible for the doings of others and everyone was to get what he worked for.

"That no soul laden bears the load of another, And that a
man shall have to his account only as he had laboured,
And that his labour shall surely be seen, Then he shall
be recompensed for it with the fullest recompense."[1]

Sin : An occasional Lapse

This was a message of salvation for man which gave him a
new confidence in himself and his ability to chart out his destiny.
He applied himself, as a result of these teachings, with a renewed
vigour, confidence and determination to shape up his own life
and brighten the future of humanity.

Prophet Muhammad (peace be upon him) announced that
sin is an occasional lapse. Man errs owing to his ignorance or
foolishness; at times he is misled by his own desires or the
machinations of Satan, Man is not sinful by nature and
hence it is typical of him to express remorse and contrition
after committing a mistake. To be regretful of one's sin and to
make up one's mind not to repeat it again is, indeed, the patri-
mony of Adam.

Merit of Repentance

The Prophet of Islam opened the gate of repentance for the
sinners and invited them to seek pardon from God for their temporary deviations from the right path. He told man that to be
broken in spirit by a sence of guilt and to seek forgiveness of
God showed the goodness of human nature and attracted the
mercy of the Lord. He laid so much emphasis on it that the
holy Prophet came to be known as the 'Apostle of Repentance.'
He told that seeking forgiveness of God was not a temporary recourse to make amends but an act of devotion to God through
which one could attain sublimity of spirit envied by those who
were elects and perfect in spirit.

Describing the clemency of God who is ever willing to
forgive the sinners, the Qur'ān employs an alluringly charming

---

1. Q. 53 : 38-40

diction inviting those who have deviated from the path of virtue
to return to God and seek His help and forgiveness and tells
them that sympathy, magnanimity and mercy of God are always
at hand for exoneration of the sins committed by man. Anyone who reads this verse of the Qur'ān will not fail to mark the
loving care of God for man.

> "Say: O! my people who have been prodigal against
> themselves,
> Despair not of the mercy of Allah;
> Surely Allah forgives sins altogether; Surely He is the
> All-Forgiving, the All-Compassionate."[1]

We find a sentiment of love and affection discernible in the
verses speaking of those who are virtuous and God-fearing.
But we find the repenters of the sins included among those
described as the elects by God.

> "Those who repent, those who worship, those who praise,
> those who fast constantly, those who bow down, those
> who postrate themselves, those who command the
> reputable and forbid the discreputable, those who keep
> God's bonds—and give thou glad tidings to the
> believers "[2]

Merit of Repentance

The place of honour accorded to those who repent for they
were the first to be mentioned among the virtuous in this verse—
alluded to the three companions of the holy Prophet who had
not joined in the expedition of Tabuk for any valid reason but
who had repented of their sin subsequently. Before the Divine
revelation referred to the condonation of the fault of these
persons, it mentioned the Prophet and the emigrants and the
helpers so that they felt no stigma attached to them after their
mistake had been pardoned. The Qur'ān, in this way, teaches
all believers to hold them in the same esteem as other

1. Q. 39: 53
2. Q. 9 : 112

companions of the Prophet.

The way these verses explain the consequences of the blotting out of sins and the elation of repentant sinners can hardly be found in the scripture of any other religion or a treatise on ethics. Now let us read these verses :

> "Allah has turned in mercy towards the Prophet and the Emigrants and the Helpers who followed him in the hour of difficulty. After the heart of a part of them wellnigh swerved aside, then turned He unto them in mercy. Lo! He is Full of Pity. Merciful for them.

> "And to the three who were left behind, until, when the earth was straitened for them, for all its breadth, and their own souls were straitened for them, and they thought that there was no refuge from Allah save in Him, then He turned toward them that they might also turn, Lo! Allah! He is the Relenting, the Merciful."[1]

The Qur'ān declares as a general rule that God's love is universal, all-embracing, while His retributive justice is restricted to particular and exceptional cases.

> "As to My mercy, it comprehends everything."[2]

A celestical Tradition of the Prophet reproduces the words of God : "Verily My mercy surpasses My anger."[3]

To be despaired of God's mercy has been declared infidelity and ignorance. Quoting Jacob and Abraham, the two great Prophets of God, the Qur'ān announces :   "No man despairs of God's mercy, excepting the people disbelieving ;"[4] and "who despairs of the mercy of his Lord save those who are astray ?[5]

A Mercy for Mankind

The misery and suffering that human race endured in this

1. Q. 9: 117-118
2. Q. 7: 156
3. *Sahih Muslim*
4. Q. 12 : 87
5. Q. 15 : 56

world because of the doctrines of inherent sinfulness of man upheld by several religions was but a feeble image of the never ending agony which awaited man in the hereafter. The monastic orders of the Medieval Ages had developed these with an appaling vividness. The humanity scared by these ghastly visions and glimpses of eternal suffering was relieved by the holy Prophet's emphasis on God's all-embracing mercy and the efficacy of repentance which infused a new life and hope in the despairing humanity.

7

Unification of Matter and Spirit · Truce between the two

Divided Humanity

Older religions, especially Christianity, had divided life into two compartments, religious and secular; and the result was that humanity had arrayed itself into two camps separated by a wide gulf in between them. Oftentimes, the two groups were at loggerheads with one another, for, the 'world' and 'religion' were to both of them incompatible spheres of human life. Every man had to choose one of the two since nobody could be expected to travel in two boats simultaneously. The prevalent view was that prosperity and progress could not be achieved without turning a deaf ear to God and the hereafter. Similarly, political power could be preserved only by saying a good-by to moral and religious imperatives. On the other hand, salvation of soul was deemed to demand taking to the life of a mendicant and recluse who kept himself away from the rough and tumble of wordly life.

The Resulting Confusion

Man is by nature easy-going as well as desirous of having wealth, honour and distinction. Any religion which disregards these innate instincts of man and makes no provision for deriving proper benefit from what are considered as wordly objects, loses **its** appeal to the intellectuals and the ambitious. Those who are practical-minded normally give preference to the worldly affairs over that of religion, if only as a social necessity and then ignore the demands of spirit. All such persons who ignore religion in this manner come to regard the division between matter and spirit as an accomplished fact. They raise the banner of revolt against the Church or the institution representing religion and deem themselves free of all moral obligations imposed by religion. A logical result of it is that the State becomes a law unto itself. The resulting struggle between the religion and the world, the Church and the State, has in the past opened the way to apostasy which has now swallowed most of the West and its camp followers.

Christian extremists were no less responsible for this sorry state of affairs since the natural demands of human instincts were regarded by them as hurdles in the way of spiritual perfection and gaining propinquity to God. The Church tried to guard itself against this instinct with savage alacrity that makes one shudder even now.[1] The result was that the enlightened sections among the Europeans developed a strong aversion to everything associated with religion. A dismal disbelief crept over the continent. The struggle between the spirit and matter intensified and ultimately no moral restraint associated with religion was tolerable to the people.[2]

The Church and State

A perpetual state of war continued between the State and the Church in Christendom during the Medieval Ages. The Church represented religion and the monastic orders while the State became an embodiment of man's material urges. The result of this struggle is too well-known : a complete division

---

1. See W. E. H. Leeky, *History of European Morals,* London, 1930.
2. See John William Drapper, *Conflict between Religion and Science,* London, 1910.

of the religious and the mundane from which the world has not recovered as yet.

Iqbal has very succinctly versified the significance of this duality of human life and its disastrous result in one of his immortal poems.[1]

"On monastic order was laid the foundation of Church,
How could mendicity contain the royalty in its confines!
The conflict was deep, between hermitry and kingship,
One was triumphant, the other subdued,
Politics got rid of religion,
Helpless was the high priest.
When the world and religion parted ways,
Avarice was the ruler, king and vizier.
Dualism made the civilization blind.
This is the miracle of a dweller of the desert,
Whose warnings reflected the tidings glad;
That for the humanity! only refuge was this,
That (the mystic) Junayd unites with Ardsher (the king)!

Islamic concept of Life

The prophethood of Muhammad (peace be upon him) converted the entire life of man into devotion to God by making the announcement that a search for the basis of all actions, religious or worldly, was what was needed to determine their worth and value. This was, in the terminology of Islamic *Shari'ah* called *niyat* or intention, which meant that every man will be judged by what he had intended.[2] Every act performed by man sincerely with the intention of abiding by the commands of God can be a means for attaining nearness to God. Everything done for the pleasure of God whether it be fighting or administration, satisfaction of the demands of human nature or earning one's living, marriage or innocent amusement was included in the ambit of religion. Conversely, all these and even the acts of devotion and worship to God became irreligious

1. Iqbal, Dr. Sir Mohammad, *Bal-i-Jibril*, Lahore, 1944.
2. *Bukhārī, Jam'i Sahīh*

if they were devoid of the intention to win the pleasure of God
and to attain salvation through them in the hereafter.

Unity and not Discord

The Prophet of Islam demolished the wedge between the
spirit and the matter and united the two belligerent camps of
religion and the world. He taught them to unite their efforts
for attaining the pleasure of God and service of humanity.
This was the achievement of the Prophet who was both a warner
as well as a messenger of glad tidings. He taught man to en-
treat God for his comprehensive welfare.

"Our Lord, give to us in this world good,
and good in the world to come, and
guard us against the chastisement of Fire."[1]

A divine revelation announced by him said :

"My prayer, my ritual sacrifice, my living, my dying—all
belongs to God, the Lord of the World."[2]

Entire Life is Devotion

The life of a believer is not made up of two separate and
conflicting instincts; it is a complete whole or a unity informed
by the spirit of devotion to God and one's responsibility to
oneself and humanity at large. The faith in God and the desire
to obey His commands show man the right path in all fields of
life provided he does not lack sincerity, virtuous intention and
desire to win the pleasure of God through the means indicated
by His apostles.

The Prophet of Islam thus converted the entire life of man
into devotion to God as if the whole world were a vast house of
worship. As the messenger of warning and cheer he united the
men forming belligerent camps who could now make a jointed
effort for the well-being of humanity since this was also a means
of winning the pleasure of God. It was because of him that the
world could see ascetics who wore crowns on their heads and
warriors who spent their nights in devotions and prayers.

1. Q. 2 : 201
2. Q. 6 : 163

8

Alliance between Religion and Knowledge

One of the distinctive features of the teachings of Muhammad (peace be upon him) was that he forged a close and pious link between religion and knowledge, made them dependent on one another and added such a lusture to the latter that it brought forth an stupendous intellectual and literary movement unparalleled in any other religion or divine inspiration during the earlier ages.

The very first revelation to the holy Prophet demonstrates the fact that the Lord of this Universe has done a great favour to mankind by bestowing knowledge on it from His presence. This initial revelation also mentions one of the greatest means of acquiring and transmitting knowledge from one individual to another, from an earlier generation to the succeeding one. The pen has always been the most widespread means for diffusion of learning since it is through it that knowledge has passed on in time and space, from one nation to another as well as from the past to the present. It is through the pen that all literary creations and libraries have come into existence.

In so far as the circumstances of this remarkable revelation are concerned, it is inconveicable that 'knowledge' should have been mentioned in the first revelation. It was addressed to an unlettered Apostle amongst the people who were backward by any standard. The pen must have been a rare commodity there for the people took pride in their illiteracy. In fact, they were known as *'ummiyin'* or the illiterates. The Qur'ān itself alludes to the situation then obtaining in Arabia in these words :

> "It is He who has raised amidst the unlettered people an apostle from among them, to recite his revelations to them and to purify them, and to teach them the Book and the wisdom though before that they were in manifest error."[1]

The Qur'ān has cited what the Jews of Madina used to say about their neighbours, the Arabs : "We are not bound to keep our faith with the illiterates."[2]

It was to these people, the nation of illiterates, that the last Prophet was sent. He was also told that :

> "In this manner We have revealed unto thee a spirit of Our command : thou knewest not what the Book was, nor what the faith. Yet We have made it a light wherewith We guide whomsoever We will of Our bondmen. And verily thou guidest to a straight path."[3]

At another place the Prophet was reminded :

> "Never have you read a book before this, nor have you even transcribed one with your right hand, for then might those have doubted, who follow falsehood."[4]

An unexpected thing

The first revelation was a remarkable event : it was the first contact between the earth and the Heaven after six hundred years when Jesus Christ had preached the Gospel to the world. Now, these initial verses did not command obedience to God nor His glorification, nor attaining His nearness, nor even forsaking idolatry or the rites and customs of paganism. These were left for later occasions and the holy Prophet was just told that :

1. Q. 62 : 2
2. Q. 3 : 75
3. Q. 42 : 52
4. Q. 29 : 48

"Read: In the name of your Lord who created,
created man from a clot of blood.
Read: Your Lord is the most Bounteous,
Who has taught the use of the pen,
has taught man, that which he did not know."[1]

This was an event of immense significance which had an important bearing on the life of humanity. This was the beginning of an era which saw the most concerted efforts being made for the promotion of learning never attempted earlier. It was the era in which Faith and knowledge joined hands for creating a new civilisation. It was an age of Faith as well as of Reason.

The command to read and acquire knowledge was to be executed under the guidance of a divine messenger and in the name of the Lord so that man proceeded ahead in his journey in the light of God's knowledge and certitude of faith. The reference to the creation of man from the clot of blood was meant to point out that man should not exceed his limits, nor feel exultant on capturing the forces of nature, since this was to come about with the acquisition of knowledge.

The pen then got the honour of being mentioned in the revelation since it has always been the most important means of learning. However, little of its significance or use was known to the then Arabs. The few men versed in the arts of reading and writing were known as '*al-kātib*'[2] or the writers. Thereafter the revelation referred to teaching of man by saying: *God taught man that which he did not know*—for God is the ultimate source of all knowledge which could enable man to know what is unknown. All the discoveries made in any field have come from this ability of man to learn and extend the horizon of his knowledge.

This was the starting point of revelation to the Prophet of

---

1. Q. 96 : 1-5
2. Only 17 persons among the Quraysh are reported to be literate, able to read and write, at that time. (Bulāzhri, *Futūh-ul-Buldān*, iv., 242). Some historians have given a few more names, yet their number was very small.

Islam which had a deep impact on the subsequent course of attaining knowledge, preaching God's message and the modes of thought. It made knowledge a fellow and ally of religion that always helped man in solving new social and cultural problems. The religion, on the other hand, was thereafter never frightened and timid in the face of knowledge.

Religions frightened of knowledge

There have been religions whose victory lay in the defeat of knowledge. This is best illustrated by an allegory relating to Prophet Solomon who had been given power over the wind. Once the mosquitoes complained to Prophet Solomon that they were disturbed and made to flee by the wind. Prophet Solomon ordered the wind to present itself but when it came the mosquitoes were no more present. He thereupon remarked how he could decide the issue in the absence of the claimants. This is true of many religions including those of ancient India. The religious leaders of old also furnish similar examples.

The struggle between the Church and knowledge in Christendom is too well-known. An American writer, W. E. H. Drapper has documented this confrontation in his famous work *'Conflict between Religion and Science.* The ecclesiastical tribunals established by the Roman Catholic Church in the Middle Ages, known as Courts of Inquisition,[1] had achieved the greatest notoriety from the number of its victims and the torture to which they were subjected. The number of their victims runs into tens of thousands. All these represent the efforts made to stall the march of knowledge in the name of religion.

Among the religious scriptures of the world the Qur'ān

---

1. These Courts were established in Italy, Spain, Germany and France for the trial and punishment of heretics. The inquisition in Spain was from 1490 under State control and practically independent of Rome. The rigour of its action began to abate in the 17th century, but it was not until 1835 that it was finally abolished. Napoleon suppressed it in Spain in 1808, and after an attempted revival from 1818 to 1820, its operation there came to an end for ever.

is unique in magnifying knowledge and holding scholars as next
to the messengers of God in dignity.

A few of such verses read :

> "God bears witness—and also the angels and those endowed
> with knowledge—that there is no God but He, the
> maintainer of equity. There is no God but He, the
> Mighty ; the Wise."[1]

> "O my Lord, increase me in knowledge."[2]

> "Are the wise and the ignorant equal ?"[3]

> "God will raise up in ranks those of you who believe and
> are endowed with knowledge."[4]

> "Even so only those of His servants fear God who have
> knowledge."[5]

The Prophet of Islam always emphasised the importance
of knowleage. He is reported to have said :

> "A scholar is superior to an ascetic in the same way as I
> am to the meanest of you."[6]

> "The scholars are the heirs of the Prophets who do not
> leave behind them dinars and dirhams. Knowledge is
> their inheritance and one who acquires it gets the
> largest share (of inheritance)."[7]

The encouragement given to the pursuit of knowledge by
Islam generated a popular enthusiasm which encompassed all
fields of knowledge and made significant contribution to its
advancement as we see it today. A European writer who has
studied the culture of the Arabs says that :"

> "The zeal exhibited by the Arabs in acquistion and pro-
> motion of knowledge was exceptionally admirable.
> Other nations can claim to have sl own a similar
> keenness for knowledge, but none could surpass them.

1. Q. 3 : 18
2. Q. 20 : 114
3. Q. 39 : 9
4. Q. 58 : 11
5. Q. 35 : 28
6. *Tirmidhi*
7. *Abū Dāwūd; Tirmidhi*

Whenever they captured a city, the first thing they did was to have a mosque and a school there. Bigger cities used to have several schools. Benjamin De Towwel who died in 1173 states that he saw twenty colleges in Alexandria, Apart from these schools the bigger cities like Baghdad, Toledo, Cordova had universities fully equipped with workshops for research. observatories, magnificient libraries, etc Spain had seventy public libraries.

"As the Arab historians say Al-Hakīm-II had a collection of six hundred thousand books in his library at Cordova and forty-four of its volumes contained the list of books in the library. Someone has rightly remarked that when four hundred years after that Charles the Wise established the first national library in France he could procure only nine hundred works and the books on religion were not enough to fill in a single almirah."[1]

Integration of knowledge

More significant than extending the frontiers of knowledge and creating a zest for its cultivation was the contribution of Islam in integrating the different disciplines of learning and guiding them to play a more positive, constructive role for the service of humanity.

Before the rise of Islam the chain of knowledge was disjointed, dispersed : findings of various branches of knowledge were very often conflicting and contradictory. Philosophy and physics were at odds with religion. Even the objective sciences like mathematics and medicine at times led to negative and athiestic conclusions. The Greek philosophers of antiquity, who remained pioneers of philosophy and mathematics for several centuries, were either pagan or athiest with the result that the knowledge of the Greeks and their way of thought were

---

1. Syed Ali Bilgrami, *Tamaddun ʻArab* (Urdu translation of Gustave Le Bon's *La civilization des Arabes*), pp. 398—99.

deemed as dangerous by the revealed religions. Islam as the religion of Unity forged a link between all branches of knowledge in order to unite them in a common cord. This achievement of Islam was made possible since it had made the right beginning. It took its first lesson from *read in the name of thy Lord who created*, which meant placing full reliance in God. More often the right beginning of a thing is a guarantee for its right conclusion. Islam thus discovered a unity with the help of the Qur'ān and faith in God, which integrated all the units. This unity constituted the true knowledge of God as promised to the believers.

> "And (who) reflect upon the creation of the heavens and the earth : 'our Lord, thou hast not created this in vain. Glory be to Thee' Guard us against the chatise-ment."[1]

The phenomena of nature often appear to man as capricious and contradictory ; they make him anxious and astonished ; sometimes they lead man to deny the existence of any Creator whom he could hold responsible for the sufferings caused by natural calamities. But Islamic knowledge guided by the Qur'ān and belief in God, solved these contradictions by pointing cut to the 'Will' of God as the sole author of all happenings and events. A German philosopher-historian, Herold Hoffding, has described the effective role played by the Unity of Cause in giving a new fillip to advancement of knowledge in his *History of Modern Philosophy* in these word :

> "The theology of a monotheistic religion is based on the fundamental thought that there is one single cause of all things. Apart from the grave difficulties which this thought involves, it has the important and valuable effect of accustoming men to abstract from differences and details and of preparing them for the acceptance of an interconnecting link of all things according to law. The Unity of Cause must lead to the unity of the law.

---

1. Q. 3 : 191

The Middle Ages educated man to this thought, to which the natural man overpowered by the manifoldness of phenomenon and inclined to polytheism, does not feel himself drawn."[1]

The Qur'ān changed the way of human thought by emphasising the Unity of Cause: it prompted man to strive to reduce varied phenomena to a single principle It incessantly called attention of its readers to the splendid marvels, the mysterious phenomenon of universe and the unitary principle governing it. This was indeed a revolutionary concept which had a far-reaching impact on the development of knowledge. I will cite here an orientalist not very sympathetic to Islam, who had to acknowledge this gift of Islam. In his Introduction to the translation of the Qur'ān by J. M. Rodwell, Rev. G. Margoliouth states :

> "The Quran admittedly occupies an important position among the great books of the world. Though the youngest of the epoch-making works belonging to this class of literature, it yields hardly to any in the wonderful effect which it produced on large masses of men. It has created an all but new phase of human thought and a fresh type of character."[2]

The force of this current of Quranic thought can be seen by the variety of forms in which it has found expression. Its achievements in the domain of knowledge have been acknowledged by several other western scholars also. Hartwig Hirschfeld writes in the *New Researches into the Composition and Exegesis of the Qur'ān* :

> "We must not be surprised to find the Quran the fountain-head of sciences. Every subject connected with heaven or earth, human life, commerce and various trades are occasionally touched upon, and this gave rise to the production of numerous monographs forming commen-

---

1. Herold Hoffding, *History of Modern Philosophy*, p. 5.
2. Introduction to *The Koran* by J. M. Rodwell, London, 1918.

taries on parts of the holy book. In this way the Quran was responsible for great discussions, and to it was indirectly due the marvellous development of all branches of science in the Muslim world......This again not only affected the Arabs, but also induced jewish philosophers to treat metaphysical and religious questions after Arab methods. Finally, the way in which Christian scholasticism was fertilized by Arabian theosophy need not be further discussed.

"Spiritual activity once aroused within Islamic bounds was not confined to theological speculations alone. Acquaintance with the philosophical, astronomical and medical writings of the Greeks led to the pursuance of these studies. In the descriptive revelations Muhammad repeatedly calls attention to the movement of the heavenly bodies, as parts of the miracles of Allah, forced in the service of man and therefore not to be worshipped. How successfully Moslem people of all races pursued the study of astronomy is shown by the fact that for centuries they were its principal supporters. Even now many Arabic names of stars and technical terms are in use. Medieval astronomers in Europe were pupils of the Arabs.........In the same manner the Quran gave an impetus to medical studies and recommended contemplation and study of Nature in general."[1]

1. Hartwig Hirschfeld, *New Researches into the Composition and Exegesis of the Quran*, London, 1902, p. 9.

9

Intellectual pursuit in Religious matters

Earlier Religions

We are not aware of any religion or scripture, claiming its origin to revelation or inspiration, which has urged its followers, in the way the Qur'ān does, to make use of their faculties of knowing and reasoning, take lessons from past experiences, observe the multiplicity of phenomena in order to reflect over them, and called them to account for their mindlessness in ignoring harmony between the laws of nature and working of the universe or for paying little heed to episodes of the past.

Seeing and understanding

Among and senses possessed by man the Qur'ān very often appeals to the sense of seeing so that he may observe carefully in order to understand the nature of things. Here are a few examples.

> "Have they not seen how We drive the water to the dry land and bring-forth crops therewith, whereof their cattle and themselves eat ? What, will they not see ?"[1]

> "But blind they were, and deaf. Then God turned towards them ; then again blind they were, many of them, and

---

1. Q. 32 : 27

deaf ; and Allah is beholder of what they do." [1]

"Say : Are the blind and the seeing equal ? Will you then
not reflect ?"[2]

"The likeness of the two parties is as the blind and the deaf,
and the seeing and the hearing. Are the two equal in
likeness ? Are you not admonished then ?"[3]

"Say: Are these, the blind and the seeing alike, or are
darkness and light alike ?"[4]

"Not equal are the blind and the seeing, neither darkness
and light."[5]

The Qur'ān warns man for being headless and unreflecting
on the natural phenomena which are but signs of God.

"How many a sign there is in the heavens and in the earth
that they pass by turning away from it."[6]

"Therefore take head, you who have eyes !"[7]

In order to emphasise the need for applying one's mind, the
Qur'ān very often uses such expressions 'haply you will reflect',
'Do you not understand' and 'if you will reflect'. Such phrases
have been employed at as many as 23 places.

"So Allah makes clear His signs for you : haply you will
understand·"[8]

"Verily We have expounded you the signs, if you will
reflect."[9]

"Abode of the hereafter is better for those who are God-
fearing. Do you not then understand ?"[10]

"And assuredly We have sent down to you a Book in which

1. Q. 5. : 71
2. Q. 6 . 50
3. Q. 11 : 24
4. Q. 13 : 16
5. Q. 35 : 19-20
6. Q. 12 : 105
7, Q. 59 : 2
8. Q. 2 : 242
9. Q. 3 : 118
10. Q. 7 : 169

is a admonition for you;   Will you then not reflect."[1]
"And you pass by them in the morning and in the night;
    will you not understand ?"[2]

Those who are doomed to hell are particularly reproached
for not using their intellect.

"They (also) say : If we had only listed or had understood,
    we would not have been of the dwellers of the Blaze."[3]

At more than twenty places the Qur'ān speaks well of those
who use their brains.

The Qur'ān repeatedly calls attention to the need of giving
thought; praises those who are thoughtful and condemns those
who are unreflecting.   On eleven occasions it points out the virtue
of collecting one's thoughts and contemplating on the signs of
God·

"Who remember Allah standing and sitting and lying on
    their sides and reflect on the creation of heavens and
    the earth ;"[4]

"So relate the story, haply they will reflect."[5]

"Surely in that are signs for the people who reflect."[6]

Raking one's brain and contemplation are the means,
according to the Qur'ān, through which man can perceive the
reality.

"Our Lord ! Thou hast not created this in vain."[7]

Great influence on Human Race

The Quranic teachings gave birth to a rationalist trend in
the widest sense of the term taken etymologically and historically.
It made a deep impact on arts and literature and human civilization all over the world in such a way as if a new window had

1.   Q. 21 : 10
2.   Q. 37 : 138
3.   Q. 67 : 10
4.   Q. 3 : 191
5.   Q. 7 : 176
6.   Q. 13 : 3
7.   Q. 3 : 191

been opened to let in light and fresh air. Islam broke open the lock with which human intellect had been fastened for ages by the enemies of reason, masquerading as representatives of religion. It was then that the humanity woke up after its long sleep of several centuries, removed the hurdles placed in its way and set its foot on the road to enlightenment and progress.

A French scholar Jolivet Castelot has described this astounding achievement of Islam in his *La loi de l'histoire* (The Law of History). He writes:

"Arabs rapidly made strides after the death of the Prophet since the time was also very congenial for the spread of Islam. Simultaneously, the Islamic civilization saw a phenomenal advancement and spread in the wake of Arab victories. Sciences, arts, poetry and literature reflected its influence and thus the Arabs remained the torch-bearers of intellectualism in the succeeding centuries. They were the spokesmen of all the sciences like philosophy, astronomy, chemistry, medicine and spiritual disciplines. They were not leaders of thought, discoverers and inventors only in name but truly deserve to be so called for they applied their mind with wisdom and intelligence. The span of Arab civilization was short, yet its influence was far-reaching. We can only regret its downfall."[1]

He also says :

"Although they were feudalistic by temperament yet their accomplishments were far beyond their capacity. They gave birth to an admirable civilization. Europe is indebted to Arab civilization which helds away from the tenth to the fourteenth century. Europe imbibed its philosophical and intellectual thought which imperceptibly influenced the Medieval Ages. Compared to Arab civilization, Arab sciences and Arab literature it (Europe) appears to us sunk in ignorance and darkness—it

1. Cited from *Al-Islām Wal Hazārat-ul-'Arabiya* by Muhammad Kurd 'Alī, Vol. II, pp. 543-544

benefited from the health-giving thoughts propagated by the Arabs.

"No Civilization was there during these four centuries. Intellectuals of the West are today holding aloft the banner of this very civilization."[1]

Gustave Le Bon writes about Arab contribution to modern civilization.

"Observation, experimentation and inductive logic which form the fundamentals of modern knowledge are attributed to Roger Bacon but it needs to be acknowledged that this process of reasoning was entirely an Arab discovery."[2]

Robert Briffault has also reached the same conclusion for he says :

"There is not a single aspect of European growth in which the decisive influence of Islamic civilivation is not traceable."[3]

He further writes :

"It was not science only which brought Europe back to life. Other and manifold influences from the civilization of Islam communicated its first glow to European life."[4]

It is sometimes claimed that the renaissance of Europe owes everything to the revival of Greek thought. The renowned historian H. G. Wells, however, asserts that the modern world received the gifts of light and power from Islam.

".......From a new angle and with a fresh vigour it (the Arab mind) took up that systematic development of positive knowledge which the Greeks had begun and relinquished. If the Greek was the father, then the Arab was foster-father of the scientific method of dealing with reality, that is to say, by absolute frankness, the utmost

1. Cited from *Al-Islām Wal Hazārat-ul-ʿArabiya* by Muhammad Kurd ʿAli, Vol. II, pp. 543-544.
2. Prof. Mohd. Iqbal, *Iran ba Ahd-i-Sasaniyan*, Dehli, 1941 (Urdu translation of G. Le Bon's *La civilization des Arabes*).
3. Robert Briffault, *Making of Humanity,* p. 190
4. *Ibid.* p. 202

simplicity of statement and explanation, exact record and exhaustive criticism. Through the Arab it was and not by the Latin route that the modern world received that gift of light and power."[1]

1. H. G. Wells, *The Outline of History*, London, 1920, p. 273

10

Promotion of Justice and Morality
A Duty enjoined on Muslims

Need for Guides

The long history of human race, human psychology and the science of ethics would agree on the point that the best ideals, moral education and exemplary behaviour would not be sufficient to sustain public morality of a higher level for any length of time unless a group of persons (or, more approriately, a community) is there to invite the people to the path of virtue and goodness, always willing to strive for it and guide othcrs through its personal examples of virtuous behaviour.

This is the reason why we find that the teachings of certain prophets (let alone of reformers, moralists and philosophers) did not last long after them. They had not left devoted followers who could take up the responsibility of spreading their message, make sacrifices for it and set personal examples as norms of conduct for individual and social life of the people. They caused a ripple on the surface of society to which they belonged but their nations soon relapsed to a herd of cattle without any shepherd to guide them.

The Elect Community

The finality of the prophethood of Muhammad (peace be upon him) meant that the humanity was spared the trouble of making further search for another prophet and another scripture for its guidance. It also meant that the holy Prophet's followers were to act as preservers and custodians of moral order in God's universe ; they were to share the burden of the last Prophet in later ages. This community was. therefore, charged with the responsibility laid on earlier prophets (though they were not to receive any further revelation). The followers of the Prophet were told by God that:

> "You are the best community ever brought forth to mankind, bidding the good and forbidding the wrong, and believing in Allah."[1]

At another place they were told :

> "Thus We appointed you a community justly-balanced, that you might be a witness to the people, and that the Messenger might be a witness to you."[2]

The Prophet is also reported to have told some of his companions: "You have been sent to smoothen and not to make (life) difficult."[3]

The Prophet's companions and their descendants showed awareness of the moral responsibility devolving on them as successors of the last Messenger of God when one of them Rab'i b. 'Āmir (who had been sent as the envoy of Muslims by S'ad b. Abī Waqqās to the Iranian General Rustam) replied on being asked the reason for invading Iran : ' God has sent us so that we take such of his servants as He wills, out of the servitude of their fellow-beings to the service of One God ; conduct them from the narrowness of this world to the vastness of the other world and conduct them from the tyranny of religions to the justice of Islam."[4]

Need for a Moral Revolution

This view of life and the world was a concept of far-

1. Q. 3 : 110
2. Q. 2 : 143
3. *Sahih Bukhāri.*
4. Ibn Kathir, Imād-ud-din Abdul Fid'ā Ismail ibn 'Amar, *Al-Bidāyah-wan-Nihāyah*, Egypt, 1932, vol. VII, p. 29

reaching effect on the future course of humanity : it was a new
experience in the field of religious attitudes with revolutionary
potentials. The sixth century Christianity (or, in other times
also) was so conditioned that a few virtuous and upright men
could have hardly exerted any healthy influence on the society.
Qur'ān also speaks of the presence of a few virtuous individuals
among even the befallen Jews in earlier times.

> "Yet they are not all a like. Among the people of the Book
> there is a community stead-fast, that recite the revela-
> tions of Allah in the watches of night, bowing them-
> selves, believing in God and the Last Day, enjoining
> righteousness and forbidding indecency and vying
> each other in good works; those are the righteous."[1]

But these individuals were unable to make any impact on
their society ; they were few and far between and, at any rate,
not taken seriously by the great majority. Actually, there are
always a few upright individuals distinguished for their morals
and devotion to God. But it is never possible to fill in the
vacuum existing at the level of community and society unless
the reformative endeavour, patterns of upright behaviour and
virtuous conduct are visible at the social, community level
through an organised effort in the administration, trade and
business, and war and peace. Such corporate effort has to
become a distinguishing feature of the people for being really
effective in any society.

The companions of the holy Prophet constituted a group
trained and brought up for such a jointed effort. A German
scholar who had studied the life of these people has convincingly
portrayed their character and behaviour as reflecting the
virtues of prophethood. He writes in the *Annali dell'Islam*.

> "These men were true moral heirs of the Prophet, the
> future apostles of Islam, the faithful trustees of all that
> Muhammad revealed unto the men of God. Unto these
> men, through their constant contact with the Prophet
> and their devotion to him, there had already entered a

---

1. Q. 3 : 113-114

new mode of thought and feeling, loftier and more
civilized than they had known before ; they had really
changed for the better from every point of view, and
latter on as statesmen and generals; in the most
difficult moments of war of conquest they gave magni-
ficent and undeniable proof that ideas and doctrines of
Muhammad had been seed cast on fruitful soil, and had
produced a body of men of very highest worth. They
were the depositories of the sacred text of the Quran,
which they alone knew by heart; they were the
jealous guardians of the memory of every word and
bidding of the Prophet, the trustees of the moral heritage of Muhammad. These men formed the venerable
stock of Islam from whom one day was to spring the
noble band of the first jurists, theologians and tradi-
tionalists of Muslim Society."[1]

Eternal Guardians

The followers of Islam were thus raised as eternal guardians
responsible for guiding the humanity in its individual and social
behaviour, to promulgate justice, to bid the right and forbid the
wrong and to act as witnesses to the end of time. They were
made answerable to the resposibility laid on them.

> "O believers, be you securers of justice, witnesses for God.
> Let not the detestation for a people move you not to be
> equitable—deal justly, that is nearer unto piety. And
> fear, Allah : surely Allah is aware of what you do."[2]

This community was warned for the least dereliction in its
duty since this was to create difficulties for the humanity or
rather push the humanity towards mental and moral confusion.
This small group of persons, not exceeding a few hundred in its
initial period at Medina, was directed to build a society based on

---

1. Caetani, *Annali dell' Islam*, Vol. II p. 429, cited from T. W. Arnold,
   Preaching of Islam, London, 1935, pp. 41-42.
2. Q. 5 : 8

faith in God and brotherhood of Islam. The community was warned that :

> "If you do not do the same, there will be persecution in land
> and great corruption."[1]

Is this warning not meant for the Muslims todoy? Their numbers are great and they co stitute nations and states. For they have forsaken the duty of guiding and preaching, are no longer concerned with helping the aggrieved and condemning the aggressor, the world has to face fearsome consequences.

The Qur'ān reminds the believers of their duties and responsibilities, their obligation to act as guides and reformers and their accountability for not bidding the right and forbidding the wrong by calling their attention to the episodes of ancient nations.

> "Would that there had been, of the generations before you,
> Owner of wisdom forbidding corruption in the earth—
> except a few of those whom We delivered of them.
> And those who did wrong followed he ease they were
> given to exult in and became sinners."[2]

Iqbal has pithily expressed the underlying idea in the verses in one of his poems entitled "Advisory Council of Satan". The head of the Council is Satan who explains the danger he apprehends from the re-awakening of the Muslims. He calls attention of his advisers to the impending danger and advises them :

> Whose *takbīr* can smash the magic-house of dimensions six,
> Let not the night of man God-conscious reach the dawn.
> Keep him away from turmoil of action,
> So that he loses the game of life.
> You are safe so long as he is kept a slave
> And abandons this finite world to the care of others.
> Poetics and mysticism will suit him best,
> For they keep the world from his sight concealed.
> I shudder the moment he is awakened,

---

1. Q. 8 : 73
2. Q. 11 : 116

For his religion demands him to monitor this, terrestrial sphere.[1]

An abiding responsibility

It is thus essential that human civilization is put to screening from time to time and protected against its corrupting influences. This is necessary for two reasons. First, because all nations are contaminated by evil influences while life is never static; it is always on the move. It needs new impulses from time to time to meet its changing needs. It is sad that the corruptive forces, philosophies and movements have made the nation of Islam withdraw itself from the world's leadership.

The second reason is that the nation of Islam alone possesses the last and final celestial revelation. The entire human race can hope to be blessed through it alone. It should jealously guard the divine message possessed by it and keep an eye on the creeds and morals of other nations and prepare itself for leadership of the world. The nations live and prosper by unbroken struggle, continuous effort, sense of duty, readiness to make sacrifices and creative activity and not by the romanticism of past glory. When they withdraw themselves from the stage of leadership, they become a part of the past and are forgotten by others. It is thus unavoidable for the nation of Islam to take stock of its role as the barbinger of a message of healthy civilization and prepare itself afresh for world leadership.

1. *Bal-i-Jibril.*

11

Universal Creed and Culture

Incomparable Unity of Islam

A comprehensive unity of thought and culture, the like of which is not to be found in any other multi-national culture or society, was brougt about, and still persists, among the followers of Islam, thanks, chiefly, to their belief in Oneness of God. This creed includes, besides conviction in Divine Unity, faith in the prophethood of Muhammad (peace be upon him), the finality of his apostleship and the accountability in the life-to-come. The mental process emanating from this creed evokes unity of approach in the observation and interpretation of natural phenomenon, ideas and values, purpose of universe and finite nature of earthly life and the world. These had been sunk deep into the hearts of the followers of Islam and were clearly visible in the lives of the holy Prophet, his companions and later gene-rations in varying degrees consistent with their times, circum-stances, edification and extraneous influences. But common cultural elements have uniformally been present in all Muslim societies irrespective of the time and space in which they were located. These elements of cultural unity have been deeper, more pronounced and of a distinctive character in comparison to similar traits in other cultures.

Some Distinguishing Features

Islamic cultural unity depends, by and large, on the *shariah* and the moral norms prescribed by it, though the standards may vary in proportion to their compliance with the teachings of Islam. These apparent variations are inevitable, too, owing to the inherent variety in Muslim nations, countries, times and their political and social organizations, but each of these would be found to carry a distinctive stamp of Islam. The common features tracing their origin to Islam in all the Muslim societies can be seen in their unshaken faith in the Oneness of God, a sense of human dignity and equality, modesty and courtesy, hospitability to strangers, anxiety for hereafter, willingness to stake their lives for the cause of God, refraining from acts of cruelty even during warfare, toleration and, in their personal and family life, a consciousness for *taharah*—the ceremonial, ritual purity and purification — a concept deeper and wider than that conveyed by the word 'cleanliness. Similarly, all Muslim peoples would be found meticulous about the things like permissible and forbidden flesh of certain animals which should also fulfil the requirement of Islamic law by being sacrificed in the name of God. Another special feature of Muslim communities transcending their linguistic differences is that they normally have Arabic names which exhibit their reverence for God and love of the prophets, companions of the holy Prophet and his household members. Names like Muhammad and Ahmad are equally popular in all Muslim communities.

The religious and cultural unity of Muslim societies becomes even more distinct in religious observances and festivals. The five daily prayers are performed in all countries (according to their own timings of day and night) keeping in step with a set procedure. Anyone belonging to any country can participate in such congregational prayers, without any local guide or assistance, and can even lead the service. Friday is weekly day of special service. Quran is the only religious scripture memorised and recited in the original Arabic text everywhere.[1]

1. The Quran is 'the most widely read book in existence' according to Lamartine, *Histoire de la Turquie*, Paris, 1854, Vol. II, p. 277 ; D. G. Hogarth, *A History of Arabia*, Oxford, 1922, p. 52.

The same is true of call to prayer which proclaims the time for prayer in the same words at all places. Ramadhan is the month of fasting no matter whether it is summer or winter in any particular country. The two common festivals universally observed are the two *Ids* which attract the largest crowds everywhere. Hajj or pilgrimage to Mecca is yet another source of cultural unity for it has attracted large throngs from far off regions continuously during the long history of Islam. It has been singularly successful in obliterating all the barriers of race, colour, language and regional culture. In the same way, the usual words used for salutation throughout the world of Islam are *Assalamu alaikum* (peace be on you), while several Quranic expressions like '*Al-hamdu lillah* (praise belongs to Allah), *Masha' Allah* (as God wills), *Insha Allah* (if God wills) (*Inna lillah wa inna ilaihi rajioon* (to God we belong and to Him shall be return) are in common use everywhere.

Testimony of Western Scholars

Several scholars have noted this remarkable uniformity of Islamic culture. Here we will cite a few of their observations in this regard. Hamilton A. R. Gibb writes in the *Studies on the Civilisation of Islam* :

> "Islam is a concept which, phenomenalized in a number of linked but diverse political, social and religious organisms, covers an immense area in space and time. In different regions and epochs it has presented differing features under the impact of and in response to local geographical, social and political forces. Western Islam for example, in north-west Africa and medieval Spain, though it was clearly related to the Muslim heartlands in Western Asia and its culture was an offshoot of their culture, yet it evolved several distinguishing characteristics, some of which in turn influenced Islam in Western Asia. In other large and self-contained geographical areas, such as the Indian sub-continent and Indonesia, or the steppe lands extending from

southern Russia to the borders of China, parallel
factors produced similarly distinguishing forms. Yet,
each and all of these retain a certain easily recogniz-
able common Islamic stamp."[1]

Another student of contemporary Islam, Wilfred Cantwell
Smith, says about the cultural achievement of Islam :

"The Muslim achievement was seen as intrinsic to their faith.
They were not only victorious on the battlefield and
effective in many diverse departments of living, but
they succeeded also, and again in relatively short period
of time, in integrating life into that wholeness that
constitutes a culture. Many elements went into making
the Islamic civilization : elements from Arabia, from
Hellenism, from Semitic cultures of the ancient Near
East, from Sasani Iran, from India. The achievement
of the Muslims was that they welded these into homo-
geneous way of life, and also carried it forward into
new development. And it was Islam that provided the
integration, as it provided too the drive and power to
sustain it. Islamic form was given to almost every
aspect of life, whatever its content. And it was an
Islamic pattern that gave the society cohesion as well
as vitality."[2]

The Basic Ingredient

Islamic culture is dominated by its intense faith in God
whose attributes serve as the ideal to be imbibed in the individual
as well as social and cultural life of the Muslims. It is a culture
hued in the colour of Allah which makes it difficult to conceive
its institutions and organisation, nature and characteristics without its prime constituent. Whenever it has been contaminated by

1. Hamilton A. R. Gibb, *Studies on the Civilization of Islam*, London,
   1922, p. 3.
2. Wilfred Cantwell Smith, *Islam in Modern History*, New York, 1957,
   pp. 36—37.

foreign influences like national or racial chauvinism, material greed, moral decadance or social anarchy such a deviation has proved to be a temporary phase resulting from its negligence of the teachings of the Qur'ān and the *sunnah.* Nevertheless, it always tries to maintain its universalism against external and internal challenges in order to return to its original source of power as well as to realise the widest possible measure of religious social and cultural unity throughout the Islamic world. It is for this reason that the revivalist endeavour in Islam shows a remarkable continuity throughout its long history. These movements have also been very often successful in their efforts to get the community back to its moorings.[1]

Islam and the West

We have reviewed, albeit beriefly, the cultural gifts of Islam which have in the past arrested sucidical trends and put the human civilisation back on the road to progress. It would be worth-while to mention here that Islam can again exert a healthful influence on humanity but in order to repeat its performace again it must occasionally take stock of itself and get rid of the corrupting influences through a judicious intermingling of the old and the new.

Another fact that needs to be kept in mind is that Islamic culture cannot make any impact on others so long as it remains influenced by alien cultures. It cannot claim the attention of others, let alone being able to act as their guide, unless it assures its own adherents of its distinctive character containing elements of divine guidance and that it is still most suitable for all times and climes. They have to realise that it is rooted in the solid ground of the Qur'ān and *sunnah.* It prescribes a complete system of mandatory religious observances and social obligations covering a greater part of one's life and time with a set of stipulations and injunctions; for example, it does not equate purification and cultural refinement and decency with cleanliness

1. See *Saviours of Islamic Spirit* (Vols. I—IV) by the author.

and abstention from law-breaking but gives them a much deeper and wider content. It has nothing in common with the civilization of the West which has, owing to its peculiar historical development, been brought up in a materialistic, anti-religious and amoral atmosphere. Dr. Sir Mohammad Iqbal who had studied the western culture at its own centres has described it in a verse which says that "the spirits of its culture lacks sanctity."

Islamic Revivalism

It would be worthwhile to give here a quotation from my own work, a biography of the Prophet of Islam, depicting the character and morals of the people held as living models of Islamic culture, as this would be a fitting epilogue to this discussion.

> "The prophethood of Muhammad (peace be upon him) made a clean sweep of the existing order of things in the world. The longings and desires of man were now centered on a new objective; the love of God took possession of his being; the pleasure of God became the immortal thirst of human heart; mercy and kindness to God's creatures was recognised as the greatest virtue which became the sole object of man's endeavour. It was then, after the advent of Islam, that the leading feature of all the countries, Arabia and Iran, Syria and Egypt, Turkistan and Iraq, North Africa and Spain became the search for higher and tender virtues, in the pursuit of which we find thousands of love-lorn souls. During this period we see innumerable men of God preaching love of the Lord, kindness and compassion to every sentient being, merits of virtuous living, acquisition of knowledge for attaining the pleasure of God, revulsion to cruelty and indecency and emphasising the grace of humility and modesty. They taught the lesson of human dignity and brotherhood of man and made this earth a kingdom of God.
>
> "If you peep into the interior of these elevated souls, you

would witness unbelievable flight of imagination, purity of their innermost feelings and nimbleness of their percept ons. You would see how they were ever willing to put their own life at stake for others, how they made their own children and family suffer for the good of all and sundry, how they compelled the autocratic kings and potentates to do justice to the weak and the poor and how rightfully just they were even to their enemies. Of a fact it would have been difficult for us to believe today what a fine specimen of humanity, what a sublime soul were these men of God if the historians and biographers had not preserved a truthful record of their lives and doings.

"This striking change in the manner and morals of the people was, indeed, the greatest miracle worked by the holy Prophet of Islam.

"Verily God saith in truth : *We have sent thee not save as a mercy for the people.*"

---

1. S. Abul Hasan Ali Nadwi, *Muhammad Rasulullah*, Lucknow, 1979, pp. 459-60.

BIBLIOGRAPHY

English

1. Annie Besant, *The Life and Teachings of Mohammad*, Madras, 1932.

2. Arnold, T. W., *Preaching of Islam*, London, 1935.

3. Barth, A., *Religions of India*, 1921.

4. Bernier, Francois, *Travels of the Mughal Empire, A. D. 1656—1668*. (ed.) Archibald Constable, Westminister, Vol. I.

5. Briffault, Robert, *The Making of Humanity*.

6. Coulson, N. J., *Islamic Surveys : A History of Islamic Law*, Edinburg, 1971.

7. Draper, John Willam, *Conflict between Religion and Science*, *London*, 1910.

8. Devenport, John, *Apology for Mohammad and Quran*, London, 1869.

9. Dutt, R. C., *Ancient India*, 1893.

10. *Encyclopaedia Britannica* (1927)

11. *Encyclopedia of Religion and Ethics*, Edinburg, 1921.

12. Ernest De Bunsen, *Islam or True Christianity*, London, 1889.

13. Gibb, H. A. R., *Wither Islam*, London, 1932

14. Gibb, H. A. R., *Studies on the Civilisation of Islam*, London, 1922.

15. Haine, *Christianity and Islam in Spain*.

16. Herold Hoffding, *History of Modern Philosophy*, London, 1922.

17. Harwing Hirschfeld, *New Researches into the Composition and Exegesis of the Quran*, London, 1902.

18. Hogarth, D. G., *A History of Arabia*, Oxford, 1922.

19. Hughes, Thomas Patric, *A Dictionary of Islam*, London, 1885.

20. Jayaswal. *Manu and Yajnavalkya.*

21. James Carean, *History of China.*

22. Lamartine, *Historie de la Tuaquie*, Paris, 1854.

23. Lawrence E. Browne, *The Prophet of Islām*, London, 1949.

24. Lecky, W. E. H., *History of European Morals*, London, 1940

25. Macauliffe. *The Sikh Religion*, 1909.

26. Malcolm X., *The Autobiography of Molcolm X*, (ed. Alex Haley), Essex, 1965.

27. Mally, L. S. S. O., *Popular Hidusm : The Religion of Masses*, Cambridge, 1935.

28. Maryam Jameelah, *Islam Versus Ahl-al-Kitab*, Lucknow, 1983.

29. Nadwi, S. Abul Hasan Ali, *Islam and the World*, Lucknow, 1980.

30. Nadwi, S. Abul Hasan Ali, *Muhamad Rasulullah*, Lucknow 1979.

31. Naidu, Sarojini, *Speeches and Writings of Sarojini Naidu*, Madras, 1918.

32. Nehru. Jawaharlal, *Discovery of India*, Calcutta, 1946.

33. Parke, D. B., *The Epic of Unitraianism*, 1957

34. Pannikar, K. M., *A Survey af Indian History*, Bombay, 1956.

35. Rodwell J. M., *The Koran*, London, 1918.

36. Sevaram Singh, *Life of Guru Nanak.*

37. Shaw G. B., *Androcless and the Lion : A Fable Play*, 1920.

38. Schweitzer, Albert, *The Mysticism of Paul and the Apostles*, 1953.

39. Smith, Wilfred Cantwell, *Islam in Modern History*, New York, 1957

40. Tarachand, Dr., *The Influence of Islam on Indian Culture*, 1946.

41. Tarachand, Dr., *Society and State in the Mughal Empire*, Delhi, 1960.

42. Toyanbee, A. J., *Civilization on Trial*, New York, 1948.

43. Victor Chopart, *The Roman World*, London, 1948

44. William, H. G., *The Outline of History*, London, 1920.

45. William L. Longer, *An Encyclopaedia of World History*, 1964.

Arabic and Urdu

46. Abu Dawud, Sulaman b. Ash-ash al-Sajistani, *Ayyam ul-Arab*.

47. Abu Muslim, Abul Hasain, *Al-Sahih Muslim*, Bairut, 1940.

48. Abbas Mahmud Al-Aqqād, *Al-Mirāt fil Qur'ān*, Egypt.

49. Ahmad Amin, Dr., *Zuhal Islām*, Vol. I, Egypt, 1952

50. Bukhāri, Abu Abdullah Muhammad Ibn Ismāil, *Sahih Bukhāri*, Delhi, 1334

51. Al-Baihqi, Abi Bakr Ahmad b. al-Hasan, *Sunan Baihqi*.

52. Bulādhri, *Futūh-ul-Buldān*, Vol. IV.

53. Ibn Jawazi, *Sīrat 'Umar Ibn al-Khattāb*.

54. Ibn Khaldūn . Abdur Rahmān, *Muqaddmah Ibn Khaldūn*, Matbā Bahiya, Egypt.

55. Ibn Kathīr, 'Imād-ud-dīn Abul Fida'. Ismaīl b. 'Amr, *al-Bidāyah wan Nihāyah*, Egypt. 1932. Vol. II

56. Iqbāl, Dr. Sir Muhammad, *Bāl-i-Jibrīl*, Lahore, 1944.

57. Iqbāl, Prof. Muhammad, *Iran ba-'Ahd-i-Sasāniyān*, Delhi, 1941.

58. Kurd 'Ali, Mahamūd, *Al-Islām Wal Hazarat-ul-'Arabiah*, Vol. II

59. Al-Muttaqi 'Alā-ud-din 'Ali Hosām-ud-din, *Kanzul 'Ammāl*, Hyderabad, 1313 A. H.

60. Nadwi, Syed Sulaimān, *Sirat-un-Nabi*, Azamgarh, n. d., Vol. IV

61. Trimidhi, Abi 'Isā Muhammad b. 'Isā, *Al-Jāimi al-Sahih*.

9 788119 024834